JAPAN

JAPAN

Originated and developed by
NEBOJSA BATO TOMASEVIC

Text by
MICHEL RANDOM and **LOUIS FREDERIC**

Design by
MIODRAG VARTABEDIJAN

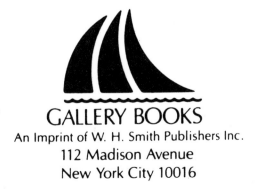

GALLERY BOOKS
An Imprint of W. H. Smith Publishers Inc.
112 Madison Avenue
New York City 10016

A Motovun Group Book

© 1986 Flint River Publishers Ltd.,
New York

ISBN 0-8317-5134-7

Translated by
Alexandra Campbell

Photography:
Vision International (London): 1-5, 7, 8,
12, 14, 15, 24, 27, 30, 38-40, 43, 54, 61, 62,
73, 91, 92, 94, 95, 98, 103, 108, 123, 139,
157, 159, 162, 165, 168
Shogakukan (Tokyo): 6, 9, 41, 44, 45, 48,
51, 52, 53, 57, 58, 90, 96, 100, 102, 104, 109,
119, 126, 130, 145, 160, 161, 167
CameraPix-Hutchison Library (London):
10, 32, 46, 47, 49, 63, 64, 72, 110, 111, 117,
120, 121, 125, 131, 132, 137, 138, 140, 144,
146, 149, 150, 155, 156, 158
Miroslav Trifunovic: 11, 13, 16, 21, 25, 26,
28, 29, 31, 33-37, 60, 65, 66, 68-71, 74-89,
93, 97, 99, 101, 105-107, 112-116, 118, 122,
124, 127, 128, 135, 136, 142, 143, 147, 148,
151-154, 163, 164
Lorenzo Sechi: 17-20, 22, 23, 55, 56, 59,
67, 129, 133, 134, 141, 166
Werner Forman: 42, 50

Production and foreign rights:
John Clark

Co-production editor:
Una Nedeljković

Editorial advisor:
Jamasaki Hiroshi

Color separations:
Scala / Summerfield Press

Printed and bound in Italy by:
Grafica Editoriale, Bologna

Table of Contents

21
Land and Sea

28
The Japanese People

33
The Contemporary City

69
A Look at Japanese History

80
Ancient Architecture

109
Beliefs and Traditions

153
The Rural Scene

156
Arts and Crafts

185
Sports and Martial Arts

217
Entertainment and the Performing Arts

241
Family Life and Education

246
The Psychology of the Japanese Today

277
Cultural Heritage

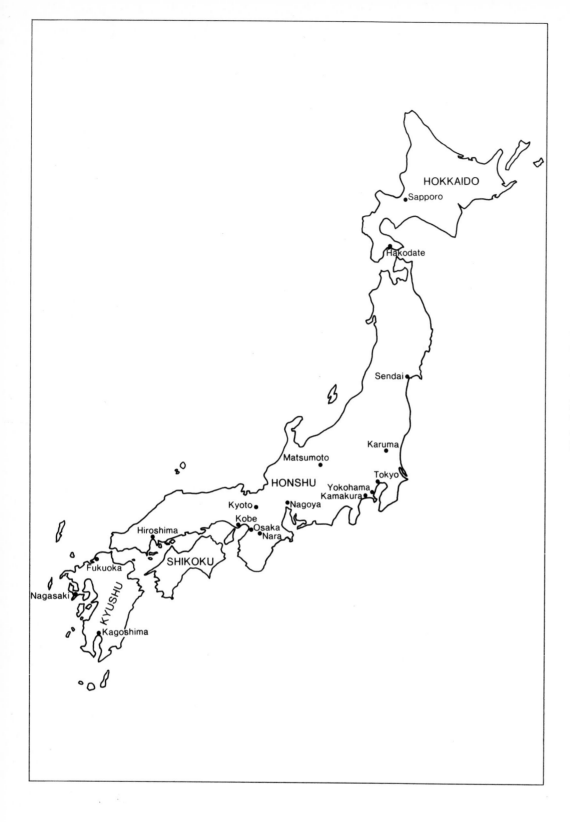

HOKKAIDO

Sapporo

Hakodate

Sendai

Karuma

Matsumoto

HONSHU

Tokyo

Yokohama
Kamakura

Kyoto

Nagoya

Kobe
Osaka
Nara

Hiroshima

SHIKOKU

Fukuoka

KYUSHU

Nagasaki

Kagoshima

1. MOUNT ASO. The largest active volcano in Japan, on the island of Kyushu. The circumference of the crater is almost 81 kilometers.

2. MOUNT SAKURAJIMA. An aerial view of the active crater and the old cone of this volcano, in Kagoshima Bay, Kyushu. Sakurajima constantly discharges smoke and fumes; its last major eruption was in 1914.

3. YUYAKE (sunset) in the area between Honshu and Shikoku.

4. YUYAKE (sunset).

5. TANCHO ZURU. The sacred cranes in Hokkaido.

6. SAKURA (cherry blossoms). The Japanese symbol of ephemeral beauty. During April when the traditional flower is in bloom, people organize picnics (O-hanami) under the cherry trees. This is not a recent habit as wood block prints from the eighteenth century show groups of people admiring the cherry blossoms at Asukayama in the hilly area just outside today's Tokyo.

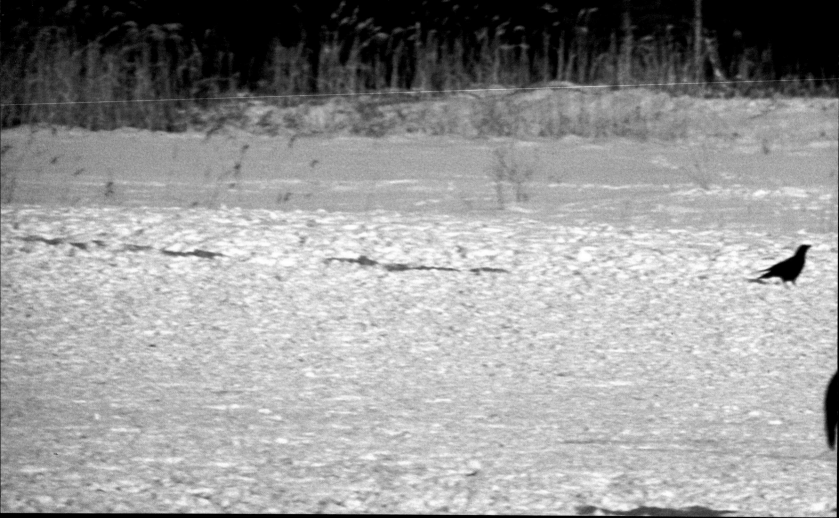

Land and Sea

J apan, land of gods and of contrasts, is first and foremost an archipelago. The sea washes round it on all sides, and to north and south a string of islands links it to the continent of Asia, like so many pillars of a bridge whose roadway has been swept away. However, the heart of Japan lies in its four main islands, Hokkaido to the north, Honshu in the center, Shikoku to the south-west and Kyushu to the south. The whole amounts to a surface area of some 372,000 square kilometers, spread over more than 3,400 mountainous islands, mostly of volcanic origin, bordered on the north-east by the Kuril Trench, over ten thousand meters deep.

These islands on the north-east of the continent of Asia are arranged in three arcs: firstly that of Honshu, which comprises the four main islands of Japan and Sakhalin Island; secondly that of the Chishima, principally made up of the Kouril Islands and Kamchatka; and thirdly that of the Ryukyu Islands, which links up with Taiwan. This last group stretches out towards the South Pacific in another arc of little islands, the Shichito Mariana, which ends in the Mariana Islands. These island arcs stake out three separate areas between themselves and the continent: to the extreme north, the Sea of Okhotsk, between the Kouril Islands and Sakhalin Island; the Sea of Japan, between Japan, Korea and Manchuria; lastly, to the south, the Yellow Sea, which washes the north-east coast of China. The four main islands of Japan lie roughly speaking between latitudes 32° and 46°, stretching over 2,000 km, but with a maximum width never exceeding 200. These islands lie very close to each other, almost interlocking, and are oriented to the south-west/north-east. Tokyo, the capital of the country, is at roughly the same latitude as San Francisco, while the northernmost point of Hokkaido is at the latitude of Montreal. In the Paleozoic age the Japanese islands were joined to the coast. It was not until the end of the Tertiary that extensive tectonic movements forced sections of the coastal range to rise up, creating a vast lake between themselves and the rest of the continent. Later, at the end of the Quaternary, subsidence occurred, gradually isolating the mountain range and breaking it up into islands. Then glacial erosion shaped the mountains, carving deep rifts in the coast. Violent volcanic eruptions disturbed the thick marine sediment and overlaid it with lava and slag. Thus the Japanese islands were formed, characterized by a mountainous backbone rising as high as 3,000 meters, and a deeply indented coastline. Because the mountains are so close to the sea, their descent is precipitous and rivers are torrential, subject to sudden floods which seriously erode the chalky soil of the limited flat ground.

7. FUJI-SAN (Fuji-Yama). West side of the mountain. Fuji is the geographical symbol of Japan and its highest peak. Climbing Mount Fuji is a religious act and every year thousands of pilgrims make their way up the mountain. The name Fuji comes from the language of the Ainu and means "mountain of fire."

Due to the narrowness of the plains lying between sea and mountain, arable and habitable land is in short supply, representing scarcely 16 per cent of the total surface area of the country. As the population of Japan has quadrupled in the last hundred years – now amounting to some 120 million – one can understand how the country has come to be so densely inhabited, reaching concentrations of 326 people per square kilometer or over 2,000 per square kilometer if one only counts habitable land. More than half the population lives in urban centers, and as these generally lie along the coast of the "belly" of Japan, an almost unbroken belt of towns links the city of Tokyo to the north of the island of Kyushu. Owing to the mountainous character of the islands, the proliferation of towns and the narrowness of the lowlands, one of Japan's essential characteristics is the general shortage of space. A further characteristic is its volcanic nature. Japan forms part of the volcanic belt of the Pacific. It consists of 265 volcanoes, of which over 50 are active and known to have erupted since history began. They are of all types, the most common being conical in shape, such as mount Fuji (3,776 m) which last erupted in 1708. Concurrently with volcanic activity, earth tremors are very frequent: about 7,500 are registered each year, of which only 1,500 can be perceived by man. A major earthquake is reckoned to occur once every ten years. The most catastrophic took place in 1923 in the Tokyo region, destroying the capital and the neighboring town of Yokohama.

Earthquakes and volcanic eruptions ceaselessly modify the physiognomy of the Japanese islands and rivers, tearing away matter from valleys, sometimes forming deltas which extend the plains and reduce the surface of the lakes. The alluvial soil, whose substratum is water-logged, and on which numerous cities rest, is particularly susceptible to movements of the earth's crust. Due to the tapping of water in the sub-soil, the city of Tokyo is subject to constant subsidence, leaving its low-lying areas particularly vulnerable to tidal waves and typhoons which blow from the Philippines, generally in September, ravaging the Pacific coast. Further modifications of the coastline are brought about by man, who is increasingly building industrial complexes on the underwater coastal shelf. On the other hand, as the steep mountain slopes are uninhabited, the forests have been to a large extent protected, providing the islands with a supply of water of which they are very much in need. But these forests are nonetheless vulnerable, being nourished by a layer of mould and humus that is often very thin. In times of heavy rain or typhoons, landslides are frequent.

It is in large part to this chronic instability of the terrain which they inhabit that the Japanese owe their character, inclined to the immediate enjoyment of whatever life may bring their way, in the knowledge that everything here below, to take a Buddhist saying dear to the Japanese heart, is impermanent, ephemeral, evanescent, "floating" (*Ukiyo*).

The four principal Japanese islands are, for all these generalizations, very different one from another, each having its individual character. Hokkaido (formerly called Ezo), although fairly large in size (78,509 square kilometers), has a relatively small population. This is partly explained by the vast mountain block that occupies virtually the whole island, but the main reason is its harsh Siberian type climate. Not colonized until the nineteenth century, it numbers barely six million inhabitants. Three-quarters of its surface is covered in forest. Snow falls in abundance, as much as ten feet deep, and icy winds constantly sweep the western coast, which looks towards Manchuria. In the plains the main crops are wheat and barley, as it is only possible to grow one crop of rice per year. Grasslands are given over to horses and cattle. Forests, mines and fish are the island's main natural resources. Sapporo, the capital, site of the winter Olympics in 1972, numbers barely one and a half million inhabitants. It developed principally after 1890, when American agricultural experts came to advise on a rational distribution of land and to apply new farming techniques. Unlike the majority of Japanese towns, its roads intersect at right angles. Several national parks have been established in this large island in a move to preserve its flora and fauna. On the coast there are some good ports, one of which, Hakodate, was from the nineteenth century frequented by the Russians. The landscape of Hokkaido is not unlike that of Canada in its distribution of land and farms.

Kyushu, the island lying at the extreme south of Japan, has an area of 41,947 square kilometers and enjoys a sub-tropical climate. Relatively heavily populated (over 15 million inhabitants), its north coast is linked to the main island by a long underwater tunnel, the *Kanmon*. At the tunnel entrance, centered on the town of Fukuoka, a huge industrial conurbation has grown up, Kita-Kyushu, opposite Shimonoseki: its industries include coal, ships, textiles, chemicals, steel-works, cars, railways. Also very mountainous – though its peaks do not scale the heights of those in Honshu – this island has a few active volcanoes, the most remarkable of which are Mount Aso, with five peaks (1,320 to 1,593 m) and a huge crater over 20 km in diameter, and Sakurajima (1,113 m) in the Kagoshima bay, which last erupted in 1914. An abundance of hot springs draws visitors in large numbers. Tropical fruits, such as bananas and pineapples, flourish on the island, as does sugar-cane. Rich in historical remains, Kyushu witnessed the development on its northern coast of the first rice cultivation in Japan and had dealings from an early date with Korea and China. It was on this same coast in 1274 and 1281 that the Mongols twice attempted, in vain, to gain a foothold, and at Kagoshima, in 1549, that Francis Xavier landed and started to convert the natives to Christianity. The Amakusa islands, linked to the mainland by five great bridges, still bear witness to the banning of Christianity in the archipelago at the beginning of the Edo period. Nonetheless Kyushu remains today one of the main centers of Christianity in Japan. Nagasaki, destroyed in August 1945 by the second atomic bomb, is today a large port with an important shipbuilding industry. The little island of Deshima was the only place during the period of Japan's reclusion from the rest of the world where foreigners, in this case the Dutch, were allowed to live. The island is now divided into nine prefectures, from which it gets its name, which means "nine provinces."

Shikoku, "four countries," is the smallest of the four main islands, having an area of only 18,758 square kilometers, and a population of some five million. It is also the least developed of the islands, perhaps because of its poor soil and very mountainous terrain (highest peaks are Mount Tsurugi, 1,950 m, and Ishizuchi, 1,980 m). It is known chiefly for its fishing. Industry, concentrated around the city of Matsuyama, is based mainly on chemicals and light engineering. The islanders also produce salt and are reputed for their handcraft of hemp wares and textile dyeing. This is a predominantly agricultural region, little visited by tourists, and still something of a poor relation to the other islands.

The main island, Honshu, is also the largest, measuring over 1,350 km in length. It is divided into three broad regions which are, from north to south, North-east Japan, including *Tohoku* and *Kanto* (Tokyo region), Central Japan and South-west Japan. These last two include the *Hokuriku*, on the coast of the Sea of Japan, the *Tosan*, in the center, the *Tokai*, on the Pacific Ocean, on the one hand; and on the other, the *Chugoku*, on the Sea of Japan and the Inland Sea (Setonaikai), and the *Kinki* (Kyoto region). Each of these districts has its particular orographic and climatic characteristics. Honshu as a whole covers 230,300 square kilometers and is the most densely populated island in the country. However, the Japanese differentiate between the reverse or "back" of the island (the part bordering the Sea of Japan) and the obverse or "belly" facing the Pacific and the Inland Sea, which alone accommodates over half the population of the entire country and is the site of all the most important cities as well as the major industries.

To the north lies the Tohoku region, crossed by a backbone of mountains. Little visited by tourists, the region is nonetheless renowned in history for its landscapes, such as Matsushima, "the islands of pines," on the Pacific coast not far from Sendai. The climate in this region is severe and the land largely given over to forest and agriculture. It is in these mountains that the main ski resorts and climbing centers are situated. The country people are known for the craftmanship of their work in wood and for the cultivation of fruit trees. The rare coastal plains are sown with rice.

The Kanto is the largest plain in Japan. In the thirteenth century it witnessed the rise of warrior clans who were destined to keep the islands under their yoke for seven centuries. It is here that Tokyo, the present capital, is situated, with its satellite towns Yokohama and Kawasaki, together accommodating some fifteen million inhabitants. The plain rises up in the north to meet the central mass of volcanic mountains that mark the end of the great Tohoku cordillera.

The Tokai is an intermediate maritime region running from the Izu peninsula to the small industrial plain of Nagoya. To the north of it lie the Tosan and the Hokuriku regions, the latter stretching along the coast of the Sea of Japan and including the Noto peninsula. It is a relatively poor area, mountainous and inaccessible, known mostly for its agricultural produce and handicrafts.

The Kinki is the historic heart of Japan. Centered on the imperial city of Kyoto, the ancient city of Nara and the vast industrial and commercial complex of Kobe and Osaka, it extends round a wide bay giving on to the Pacific and the Inland Sea. Osaka could fairly be called the Venice of Japan, so numerous are the canals that cross it. The site of the International Exhibition in 1970, it is the largest commercial center in Japan after Tokyo. At a crossroads of routes over both land and sea, the town developed particularly from the end of the sixteenth century following the surge in trade at this period in rice, silk, sake, tea and works of art; and also as a result of the flowering of the arts, theater and wood engraving to satisfy the tastes of the new merchant bourgeoisie. The Kinki was also the ancient seat of the court of Yamato, the first Japanese empire, founded to the south of lake Biwa, the largest lake in Japan. Its hills are scattered with historic monuments: the great burial mounds (*kofun*) of the first princes of the imperial line, sites of famous battles, temples, castles and ancient cities. It is here that the best tea is grown, the finest silks are woven, the most delicate of paintings and sculptures see the light of day. A great many traditions are rooted in the Yamato region, which lies close to the heart of all Japanese.

Lastly there is the Chugoku or "land in the middle," crossed lengthwise by a chain of mountains with summits which do not rise above 1,400 meters. Its south coast borders the Inland Sea, whose surface is scattered with thousands of picturesque islands and is the domain of both fisherman and tourist. Its famous sites are legion, Itsukushima, for example, or the old feudal town of Kurashiki. The northern part, bordering the Sea of Japan, is arid and known above all for its immense sand dunes, near Tottori, or the Oki islands with their fantastical colors. To the south of Chugoku, set in a magnificent bay, the tragically famed city of Hiroshima is situated; it suffered the distinction – if one can call it such – of being the first city to be destroyed by atomic bombs, on August 6, 1945. Now entirely rebuilt, it is a thriving industrial town. Opposite Kita-Kyushu, to which it is linked by a tunnel, is the town of Shimonoseki, site of the signing of the treaty which brought an end to the Sino-Japanese war in 1895.

All around these four main islands other ones lie scattered, as if forming a protective cordon. The best known are the Ryukyu islands, an archipelago stretching to the south of Kyushu, composed of hundreds of islands, the largest being Okinawa, site of terrible battles at the end of the Second World War. The other islands, little inhabited and tropical in climate, devote themselves to fishing and the cultivation of tropical crops, such as sugar cane and bananas.

The climate

As a result of its extreme length and its tortuous and compartmentalized relief, Japan experiences many types of climate, which vary according to latitude, altitude, exposure of the mountain slopes and direction of the ocean currents. The overall climate of the islands is influenced by the Eastern Asiatic monsoon. The distribution of atmospheric pressure over land and sea is radically different in winter and summer. In winter, cold currents of air coming across the Sea of Japan from Siberia chill the atmosphere considerably, especially north-west of the cordillera, while in summer, currents of warm air blow from the Pacific and warm the south-east facing slopes of the same cordillera. There is also a winter monsoon (of dry polar air), which confronts masses of humid air coming from the Pacific. The Pacific coastline is warmed by a strong ocean current, the *Kuro-shio*, while the northern coasts of the islands are permanently washed by the waters of a different, cold current coming from the North Pole, the *Oya-shio*. These currents run into each other to the east of Tohoku, creating conditions very favorable to fish breeding. The fishing grounds around the Oya-shio to the north of Hokkaido are the subject of constant dispute between Japanese and Russian fishermen.

While precipitaton is at its lowest in winter in Hokkaido, it is at its maximum from June to October throughout the islands. Kagoshima has an average rainfall of 400 mm in June, Tokyo 150 mm in July and August, and Sapporo a mere 100 mm in the same period.

Japan experiences four very distinct seasons. In olden times the Japanese started to reckon them from the time of the flowering of the cherry trees: March 30 in Kyushu, April 10 on the heights of the

Chugoku and Tosan, April 20 in the Tohoku and from May 10 to 30 in Hokkaido. The four Japanese seasons are *Haru* (spring) starting at the beginning of February, *Natsu* (summer), *Aki* (autumn) and *Fuyu* (winter). The rainy season, *Bai-u*, lasts generally from June 15 to July 15 and is followed by a month of extreme humidity. However, in the Tohoku region and in Hokkaido the effects of the *Bai-u* are hardly felt at all. The season of cyclones and typhoons blowing from the Pacific starts in August and ends in late September. The typhoons sometimes prove very destructive, as much to crops as to buildings. The best time of year to visit Japan is, then, in the autumn, between late September and late November: the air is cool, gentle, and touched with a light mist which softens the distances and brings the planes into relief. The winter, which is very harsh in the north, is relatively dry in Tokyo, over which an icy wind from Siberia, the *Karakkaze*, sometimes blows. But in Kyoto, which is set in a punchbowl, the air is cold and humid, while in summer it becomes intolerably hot and humid. It must however be borne in mind that, overall, Japan experiences an infinite number of micro-climates which modify the general climatic tendencies. From one valley to another in the space of a few miles, temperature and humidity can entirely change.

The flora obviously adapts itself to climatic variations, whether local or general, and is equally affected by altitude. The forests, which cover over half the land area of Japan, fall into three zones: the subtropical (oaks, broadleaved evergreens, camphor trees, maples, pines) where average temperature ranges from 13° to 21° Centigrade; the temperate (from 6° to 13° C) with deciduous trees, Japanese oak, cedar, birch; and the subarctic (minus 6° C) with mixed forest and conifers.

Fauna, once found in abundance, is now rare, particularly in the case of large mammals. A few mouflon live in the high mountains of Honshu and a few black and brown bears are still found in the Tohoku and Hokkaido. There are, on the other hand, plenty of badgers (*Tanuki*) and foxes, as well as hare and wild boar. A few colonies of rhesus monkeys live in Kyushu. There is a greater variety of bird-life, as many migratory species visit Japan and, among others, one finds swallows, cuckoos, swans, wild geese, pheasants and ducks. Cranes, which are a symbol of Japan, were once very common but have now become rare.

There is little grassland in Japan, dwarf bamboo (*Sasa*) often growing in the place of pasture, especially in the north. Sasa fields provide no forage for sheep (of which there are few) or cattle, for whom special grazing is provided.

*Jomon urn with typical "corded pattern"
decoration. National Museum, Tokyo.*

The Japanese People

Ethnic origin and composition

The precise origin of the Japanese people, or at least its most ancient constituents, is subject to controversy, in the absence of incontestable documents. It is nonetheless certain that the first men who populated what is now the Japanese archipelago came from the continent, at a period when the islands were still attached to the mainland by natural land bridges – in other words at least ten thousand years before Christ. The remnants of lithic industries have been found, in very small number it is true, in the layers of earth beneath those containing pottery shards, and they correspond in workmanship to what is commonly found from the Paleolithic age. But this is not sufficient to date them. At most one can say that these tools of chipped stone antedate the earliest evidence of the manufacture of pottery in Japan. This pottery seems very ancient, but prehistorians cannot date it more exactly than between 11,000 B.C. and 5,000 B.C., which is undoubtedly vague. However, it is unthinkable that such primitive men could have managed to cross the straits at a more recent date. Where did the first Japanese come from? North China? Korea? Eastern Siberia? Nothing justifies one hypothesis more than another. It is, however, probable that the first Japanese were different from the Ainu, who seemed to have arrived before them from the north, therefore across Siberia, at a remote period when Sakhalin island was not separated from the continent. (It is still no more than a few miles from the mainland, cut off by a shallow strait which freezes in the winter, allowing easy passage). The Ainu's ancestors might, indeed, have been able to cross this passage in relatively recent times. The Ainu were the last representatives of a vanished people, probably of alpine origin, who in the course of the centuries followed the retreat of the glaciers in pursuit of game. They would thus have reached Sakhalin (perhaps driven back by the Paleo-Siberians) and, being trapped, could only move in a southerly direction, thus arriving in northern Japan where they settled, keeping their customs and ethnic character up to the beginning of the last century. This hunting people, who worshipped the bear and the spirits of nature, has now virtually disappeared as a result of intermarriage with men and women from the southern islands of Japan. Pushed back into Hokkaido and to Sakhalin in the Edo period, the Ainu, perhaps former inhabitants of the coast of east Siberia, adopted the customs of nordic people like the Eskimos, while nevertheless retaining some of their individual characteristics. They differed from the Japanese in their tanned complexion, in having a round face, a nose fairly wide at its base, high cheek-bones and above all a pronounced hairiness. Their present customs do not go back more

*Dotaku with zig-zag pattern decoration,
from the Yayoi period (second-third
century A.D.). National Museum, Tokyo.*

than a few centuries and have been heavily impregnated with Japanese concepts. Having occupied a good part of Honshu up to the sixteenth century and clashed with the other inhabitants of the islands, they had numerous contacts with them, resulting in much intermarriage. Their blood mixed with that of the southern Japanese and noticeably modified their ethnic make up, while the Ainu race became increasingly Japanized and in the course of the last few years has virtually disappeared. There are barely a few dozen families in Hokkaido who are truly Ainu.

It seems that in prehistoric times in south Japan the first arrivals were joined by others from China, Korea, perhaps even Melanesia, these last arriving via Taiwan and the Ryukyu islands. The primitive people of Japan, known by the name Jomon (meaning "corded pattern," from the marks that decorated the pottery, a technique that probably originated in Siberia) were already a fairly heterogenous mixture when, at about the beginning of the third century B.C., new peoples arrived via Korea, possibly from south China, and installed themselves in the north of Kyushu. These peasants brought with them the technique of rice cultivation, previously unknown to the hunting and fishing Jomon people. They also brought iron tools, the technique of weaving vegetable fibers and a new way of burying the dead. While the Jomon seem not to have had proper funeral rites, these Yayoi (from the name of the district in Tokyo where remnants of their pottery were found) buried their dead in cists or in enormous urns of baked clay, an ancient Chinese custom. The transition from the Mesolithic culture of the Jomon to the Neolithic type culture of the Yayoi was accomplished fairly gradually as the new arrivals spread out over the islands. It is probable that there were several waves of immigration, each one bringing its own techniques, burial methods, and numerous objects, notably in bronze, as well as agrarian and more-or-less animist forms of worship. It was these "Chinese" who began to organize the country into agricultural communities. When, towards the middle of the first century A.D., with the supremacy of the Han in China, the wave of immigrations ceased, the new Japanese, cut off from their source of bronze utensils and objects, began to copy them in stone or other materials. The population was then divided into farmers, fishermen and hunters. Little by little these last took refuge in the north where, at least until the tenth century, they carried on Jomon customs and ways of life.

Towards the middle of the period, that is to say around the time of Christ, new bronze objects with a very slight percentage of tin seem to have appeared, particularly in south-west Honshu and in Shikoku, showing that new techniques had arrived, perhaps with new people from China or Korea. The villages, whose economy was based on rice culture, grouped themselves into states. Technical standards improved, houses replaced simple huts, nets were used for fishing. The injection of new blood at this period seems to have had the effect of "Mongolizing" the native population and giving it the features we know today, at least in peasant society.

Towards the middle of the third century A.D. there arrived in Japan, again in the north of Kyushu, a new people who had come from Korea via Siberia. These new immigrants were taller, had long faces, hooked noses and very fair coloring, showing affinities with North American Indians in their racial characteristics. They penetrated the archipelago in groups, mounted on large horses, and were organized into warrior clans. Clad in armor, armed with swords and powerful bows, it did not take them long to dominate the peaceful Yayoi farmers and to establish an aristocracy. They buried their dead in sarcophagi of stone or baked clay, overlaid by enormous stone tumuli, the *Kofun*. At the same time they sought to gain a foothold in south Korea and conquered a small state there, the Mimana. These newcomers mixed fairly little with the Yayoi population, but organized them into clans, giving them chiefs who were also shamans. As a result of their links with Korea, they imported elements of Taoism and Confucianism, then, extending their zone of influence, established a veritable kingdom in Yamato, to the south of present day Nara. For a time this kingdom was in military conflict with another in the Izumo region on the north-west coast, but the latter was soon brought to its knees. These mounted archers were to found a dynasty in Japan, constituting the basis of all aristocratic families and organized on the same political lines as were in existence in Korea. An entire Sibero-Korean mythology superimposed itself on the animist beliefs of the farmers, giving rise to an original form of religion based on the worship of spirits of nature, which came in time to be called Shinto. Japanese history properly speaking began around 538 with the arrival from Korea of Buddhist monks, who brought with them new building techniques and forms of government. The pottery, which in the times of the mounted archers was characterized by vases of Korean type and particularly by figurines of baked clay representing people, objects and houses (*haniwa*), then grew finer and bronze work was perfected, thanks to imported techniques and the excellence of the Japanese craftsmen. Meanwhile the "Japanese" were driven from Korea (around 663) and retreated to the islands, taking with them a large number of Korean families who settled there. The by then very numerous aristocracy of the mounted archers began to some extent to mingle with the people, infusing them with new blood.

All this mixing of peoples resulted in the Japanese of today and one can still discern among them several distinct racial types: people of peasant origin (Yayoi and descendants), who are of average size and round faced; the descendants of the mounted archers, who are taller, with slightly hooked noses; northern people, who are a mixture of Yayoi, Jomon and Ainu; a few types to be seen in south Kyushu who have Indonesian characteristics, and indeed all the intermediate stages between the main original races. The original Japanese language, that spoken in the fifth and sixth centuries, before the introduction of a large number of Chinese words, was probably the result of these racial minglings and it would be fruitless to look for its precise origin. The language was progressively modified, above all from the seventh century, by increasingly significant importations of Chinese writing and phonetics. After the tenth century, cut off for a time from direct contact with China, the language developed along strictly Japanese lines. Chinese chronicles recount that in the fifth century the people of Wa (dwarves) used the services of a type of priest-sorcerer-shaman, and took care to preserve ritual purity; they were honest and happy, lovers of song and dance, and inclined to superstition. The people tattooed their bodies and had no system of writing. They counted with the help of a square ruler or knotted cords. Polygamy was practised, or rather a form of matriarchy, and the nobles owned slaves. The Kami were worshipped (as today in Shinto) with the clapping of hands. In a great many details the Japanese of today have remained the same as those who populated the islands at that period.

*Haniwa, house with a hipped edge roof,
from the Kofun period (fourth century
A.D.). National Museum, Tokyo.*

The Contemporary City

At first sight, Japanese cities appear an inextricable tangle of ultra-modern blocks and suburban shanties haphazardly set along streets and alleys, without the slightest regard to town planning. The newly arrived visitor stands bewildered and lost, wondering if he will ever manage to get his bearings. His sense of unease is only compounded by the multiplicity of main roads criss-crossing the city, soaring over houses, rising in tiers one above another. And as almost all signs are, naturally, written in Japanese, it does indeed prove difficult to find one's way. But take comfort: the Japanese themselves are in the same predicament, even though they can read the sign-posts. When it comes to locating a specific address, it is almost as hard for them as it is for us. Because there are no street names! Only the names of areas or crossroads, followed on the address by a series of figures which mean nothing to us but in fact indicate the area code, the number of the housing block, and sometimes also that of an annex. A taxi driver is frequently obliged to stop at a *Koban* (a miniature police station situated at all main crossroads) to ask the way. The policeman on duty, who personally knows all the inhabitants of the locality in his charge, consults the map of his segment of town and gives directions. Inevitably this can take a certain amount of time, but at the end of the day one always gets there. One of the rare places where things are a little easier, most of the main roads having a name, is Kyoto. Because Kyoto was originally designed to a Chinese plan, that of the Tang capital, Chang'an, with roads intersecting at right angles: this made it essential, if people were ever to get their bearings, to name or number main roads. Tokyo, on the other hand, like most other Japanese cities, was originally a number of separate villages which came to amalgamate, though each preserved its individual character for a long time. These villages had sprung up in clusters round a castle, seigniorial residence, temple or shrine, and no formal plans were ever drawn up for their development. The only unit used in their construction was the *Cho*, that is to say a rectangle some 110 meters in length. In due course these units got broken up, were intersected by alleys, cul-de-sacs and passages which completely disrupted the primitive grid layout. A further point, when a town grew up around a castle, the nobles had no interest in seeing straight roads built: it was preferable that the approach remain difficult for any future assailant. These towns developed at a tremendous rate, in particular on the "belly" of Japan, and have ended up virtually running into each other, from Tokyo to Shimonoseki, forming a kind of Megalopolis over 900 km in length, in which half the Japanese population lives. Each city has nonetheless retained its individual character, derived from its historical beginnings. While Tokyo is organized round the old shogunal castle, Osaka is centred on the sea, which flows into the city along innumerable canals. But the actual way of life is the same more-or-less everywhere, if perhaps a little less hectic in Nara and Kyoto, which have become provincial towns. One finds in them the contrasts that typify all Japanese towns: the commercial districts with their gigantic modern buildings and wide streets; shopping areas, generally centered round railway stations; more-or-less specialist districts (in Tokyo, for example, one finds Kanda, the "Latin quarter"; Akihabara, the center for all things electronic; Ginza, the throbbing heart of the city; Marunouchi, the business district, etc.). Department stores, of which there are a huge number, are situated in the center of shopping districts, close to the railway stations. In some cases, as in Shibuya, Tokyo, the latter have been incorporated into shopping centers: one can buy socks and underwear then take the subway on the same floor of the building, or else the railway train five storeys lower down. Shops are in any case omnipresent in Japanese towns: little and large, overflowing with merchandise, they jostle each other in every street, form shopping arcades, invade the basements and upper floors of buildings, populate the corridors of the underground. One is everywhere welcomed with a smile, as courtesy to a potential customer, whether or not he actually buys anything, is a rule that suffers no exception. Most goods purchased can be exchanged and even returned without difficulty. Furthermore, shops, particularly the smaller ones, stay open late into the evening, and on Sundays. Hotels have shopping arcades with Western opening hours only, but this is an exception. In every district there are shops open late, even up to 11 o'clock or midnight. Life is equally easy when it comes to meals: restaurants, street stalls, sushi and snack bars will serve you day and night. If hungry late in the evening, you can always order by telephone from a neighboring restaurant. Your meal will be delivered immediately, whatever the hour, wherever you are staying, even if you want no more than a bowl of soup. And at no extra charge. The telephone is omnipresent in shops, boutiques, streets, subway stations, indeed everywhere and is made constant use of. It is inexpensive and, most important, enables you to telephone the person you wish to visit and ask him to fetch you when you are lost, as frequently happens. Besides booths equipped with multiple telephones, at the entrance of every shop there is an *Akadenwa*, a red box, which is actually a telephone, and available for general use. One never comes across telephones that are out of order in Japan (or very rarely) as the Japanese have an innate respect for property: no one, not even a hooligan, would dream of smashing things up purely for the sake of it. Bookshops are the most frequented of all. Throngs of people, for the most part young, crowd round the shelves, standing upright for hours, freely reading books and magazines. They may be penniless students, or simply curious minds come to wile the time away. The bookshops can be vast, stocking works of all kinds and ranging over several floors of a building. In a similar way, restaurants sometimes associate to occupy the various storeys of a building. Shops, offices and private flats are commonly found under one roof. And it is not unusual to come across shops and restaurants on the tenth floor of a modern office block. This enables the staff to eat and do their shopping without leaving the building: they have only to go up or down a few storeys. The higher buildings rise, the further they descend at basement level, and at every floor something will be going on: no space is wasted. A Japanese city is a hive of perpetual activity.

What strikes a visitor above all else, is the extraordinary diversity of the architecture. In the heart of cities where modernism is king, buildings in all styles stand side by side, ranging from the most classic to the boldest of architectural experiments. The majority of new buildings have been designed to resist earthquakes, which means that each concrete structure is reinforced by a close-set grid of welded steel wires. In case of an earthquake, the whole building will tremble, but it will not collapse. In contrast to these technical norms in the inner city, in the outskirts where people live in individual houses, styles are fantastically diverse, realizing the wildest dreams of each owner or architect. Beside a traditional house built of wood and tiles, set in a tiny garden, one may find a villa in rococo or art déco style, or a scaled-down version of a European castle, or a block of *Apato* (apartments) in which corridors and piping are placed outside to avoid any waste of space. Streets are lined with countless wood and steel posts bearing telephone lines and electric cables and transformers, which weave a kind of net against the skies. There are no proper sidewalks, just spaces alongside streets marked out by a white or yellow line. So pedestrians must make their way cautiously, along narrow roads which wind amidst posts, traffic lights and the gutters invariably lining each side of the route. These drains of cement are not always covered by a protective grill and can prove a hazard to cars on the open road, while in town they are often responsible for broken legs and twisted ankles. Apart from the main thoroughfares, which are built on Western lines, planted with trees and equipped with wide sidewalks, roads are often so narrow that two average sized cars can pass each other only by dodging in and out among the posts. Japanese car manufacturers, well aware of the problems, have helped to minimize them by designing cars of astonishing smallness. Yet one does not often see cars, of whatever size, parked the length of the sidewalk as in the West, except in rare places where this is authorized. No one has the right to buy a car unless he can show that he has a parking place at his disposal, either at home or nearby.

Since the first railway line in Japan, between Tokyo and Yokohama, was inaugurated on October 14, 1872, the construction of new lines has not ceased. Each private company has its own network, competing with rival companies in terms of speed, comfort and price. In the towns the railways make use of the tracks of the subway system and vice versa, so that the two interconnect. In rush hour, at its peak when office workers head for home, subway and railway trains follow each other almost without interval, each train (sometimes twelve carriages long) only a few hundred yards behind its predecessor. Every evening, in less than an hour, the main Tokyo station manages to handle over three million passengers. In the frequently crowded subway, officials in white gloves (everyone dealing with the public in their work, such as the police or taxi-drivers, wears immaculate gloves) have the job of helping passengers aboard by pushing them into the carriages. Despite the crowding, there is no disorderly rush: the positions of the carriage doors are marked on the platform, and passengers calmly queue in the designated place. The subway and railway systems differ little from each other. Most of the private railway networks are narrow gauge, while subway and a few other lines are standard gauge. The entire system is electrified and certain privileged lines, such as the

Shinkansen, linking Tokyo and Shimonoseki, are among the most modern and rapid in the world. Both trains and cars drive on the left, although trains occasionally take the righthand track. Cars are subject to a speed limit, including on the motorways (which are few in number because of the ruggedness of the Japanese terrain). Apart from the extensive railway network (comprising over two hundred private companies) which crosses Japan, one can travel on buses and coaches, an easy and convenient form of transport, particularly in the towns. One pays on boarding the vehicle, depositing one's fare in a little transparent box (which sometimes gives change and issues a ticket). Taxis exist in abundance (over 50,000 in Tokyo alone), and belong to numerous private companies. Their doors open and shut automatically, controlled by the driver. It is not a Japanese custom to give tips. A great many taxis are fuelled by propane gas, which is stored in a container in the trunk, leaving little space for suitcases. If one is heavily laden, it is worth taking a special taxi, which can be ordered anywhere, thanks to the ready availability of the telephone. Driving oneself, extreme care is called for, whether in town or on the highway, as traffic is always heavy and slow. Bicycles can be a pleasant way of getting about in the outskirts, visiting temples and gardens, although it would hardly be advisable to ride them in the city centers. They can easily be hired for a modest sum, except during holidays, when there is heavy student demand.

On an outing it is agreeable to stop for a break in one of the *kissaten*, or cafés, that are everywhere. All serve excellent coffee, whether large establishments or little ones with room to accommodate no more than a dozen or so customers. What is often surprising to Western eyes is the smallness of the tables and chairs, another consequence of the chronic lack of space in the country. On entering a café, or indeed any little shop, one passes a piece of material decorated or inscribed with the name of the establishment and ripped into two or three pieces. This is the *noren*, which in olden times was supposed to destroy the evil spirit from outside, preventing it from entering. Nowadays the *noren* is no more than a traditional decoration.

8. SHUTO-KOSOKU-DORO. The main highway of Tokyo.

9. TOKYO. Skyscrapers at Shinjuku.

10. TSUKUBA. Expo '85 World Exhibition, near Tokyo.

11. POTO-PIA. Building in the shape of a coffee cup, on the huge artificial island in the port of Kobe.

12. HOKOSHA-TENGOHU. Pedestrian thoroughfare in Osaka.

13

14

13. *YOYOGI PARK, TOKYO. Rock fans in the Far East.*

14. *Old and new fashions. The traditional dress of the Japanese is the kimono; the word means roughly "the thing worn." It is a commodious garment which overlaps in front of the body with neither buttons nor fastenings and is held in place by a sash worn around the waist or the hips. This sash is called an obi. For a people whose normal seated posture was either kneeling or sitting cross legged, such a loose fitting garment was indispensable.*

15. *"MOSHI MOSHI": Japanese for "hello" on the telephone.*

16. *MADO-FUKI. Washing windows in Osaka.*

17-18. YOYOGI PARK, TOKYO. *Sports hall used for the Olympic Games.*

19. *Modern Japanese reception hall.*

20

20. SHINKANSEN (the bullet train). The first line, between Osaka and Tokyo, was completed for the Tokyo Olympic Games (July 1964). Travel time between the two cities, 500 kilometers apart, is currently 3 hours and 10 minutes.

21. Japan has the most modern and efficient public transport network in the world.

21

22-23. *SHINJUKU, TOKYO. Skyscrapers. Japanese contemporary architects are among the world's finest. Their ranks include such luminaries as Tange Kenzo and Maekawa Kunio.*

24. *CHU-GAKUSEI. Secondary school pupils in traditional black uniforms.*

25. *TAKENOKO-ZOKU (street dancer). Young people meet in Harajuku, Tokyo on Sunday mornings to dance. Inspired by Western music and fashion, these youngsters show little appreciation for Japanese folk traditions, way of life or work philosophy.*

26. *SAYOKU (student of Kyoto University belonging to a radical left wing political faction).*

27. *Police protecting the wife of a V.I.P.*

28. *SENKYO (election campaign). Little interest is shown in the proceedings even in the center of Kyoto.*

29

29. *TOBA, Mikimoto Pearl Island.*
Implanting the nucleus of a cultivated
pearl.

30. *CHA-NO-YU (tea ceremony).*
Sometimes tea ceremonies are performed
in the big companies to maintain
traditional spirit and discipline. Some
Japanese feel that the loss of the "Oriental
spirit" is too high a price to pay for
modernization and the country's industrial
and commercial successes.

31

31. *Old women resting in front of a temple.*

32. *Women in Japan are mothers first: this is their traditional role and very few married women go out to work. This custom is changing slowly. . . very slowly.*

33. *"Mr Donuts" cakes are popular and can be found at all* kissaten, *as cafés are called.*

32

33

65

34

34. Children playing baseball in the suburbs of Kyoto. Among the many American imports into Japan this game is certainly one of the most popular.

35. DENSHA (local train). Kyoto suburbs.

36. NEMUTAI (sleepy).

A Look at Japanese History

The arrival of man in Japan dates from a very remote age, certainly going back to the time when the islands were still attached to the continent, which means over ten million years ago. Some stone tools found have been attributed to the Paleolithic era, but it has not been possible to assign them to a more specific period. Pottery seems to have been in use from a very early date, associated with the remaining traces of microlithic industries. It was to evolve continuously over thousands of years, almost up to the tenth century A.D. in the Tohoku and Hokkaido, though only until the third century B.C. in north Kyushu and south Honshu. This very protracted period was known by the name *Jomon*, which means "cord-patterned," because of the characteristic decoration of the pottery.

Before the end of the third century B.C. a new people appeared in north Kyushu. They probably came from south China and brought with them new techniques: the cultivation of rice in flooded fields, weaving, and tools of wood reinforced with iron. These Yayoi people (from the name of a district of Tokyo) spread over the southern half of Honshu and buried their dead in cists or great double earthenware urns, which suggests that there were Korean elements mingled with the Chinese arrivals. A great many bronzes were brought over at the time from China and soon came to be imitated in Japan and honored as sacred objects (halberds, mirrors, dotaku). The pottery at this time was finer than in the Jomon period. Fishing came into prominence and there were signs of some social organization, centered around the agricultural village. It is probably from this period that one can date the first elements of the Shinto religion, a veneration of the forces of nature. The agricultural villages organized themselves into little kingdoms, which quickly came to vie with each other for supremacy and arable land. This kind of civilization was to last for six centuries, until the dawn of the third century A.D., which saw the arrival from Korea and Manchuria of mounted archers, riding on great horses, who were soon to impose their will on the relatively peaceable farming people of Yayoi. These groups of warriors, organized in clans, dominated the people of the islands politically. They imposed on them their own legends, myths, and beliefs, which came to mingle with those of the original population, creating a veritable religion based on the more-or-less shamanic veneration of Kami (superior beings), and later to develop into Shinto. The chiefs of these Korean warriors brought with them a new form of burial, the Kofun, which were tumuli, often of great size. The use of iron developed and the warriors wore armor, which was depicted on the tubes of baked clay called Haniwa, several

37. KATA-GURUMA (sitting on the shoulders). Girl watching the Midosuji Parade from a special position.

rows of which surrounded the great tombs of the kings and other sacred sites. These tombs were sometimes decorated with symbolic paintings. Arms and jewels found inside them show a close affinity to objects usually found in Korean tombs. It was probably towards the fourth or fifth century that Chinese script began to be known in Japan, and that the Koreans introduced to the archipelago the ideas of Confucianism and Taoism, which were eventually superimposed on native beliefs. From this time forward the organization of the state was under the direction of "emperors" who controlled the minor kings (Kuni No Miyatsuko) of the land of Yamato (north Kyushu and the Kinki region). Towards the middle of the sixth century there arrived some Korean Buddhist monks who brought with them not only the first elements of their religion but also new building techniques, roofing of glazed tiles, embroidery, sculpture, and painting. The prince Shotoku (died in 622) gave Yamato – which the Chinese from then on called Japan, "land where the sun rises" and no longer Wa, "land of dwarves" – a seventeen article constitution which was to be the foundation of the entire political and spiritual development of Japan. This constitution, based on Buddhism, Confucianism and good sense, was to form the basis of Japan's first authentic government, organized on Chinese lines. The Japan of Yamato times, which had tried to regain its territories in southern Korea lost in 562, was definitely driven from the Korean peninsula in 663 and from then on concentrated on the conquest of the remaining Japanese islands and the rational organization of the people who lived there. This is the period known as Asuka, from the name of one of the first capitals of the Tenno, or emperors. Works of art and literature arrived continually from China and Korea, and were immediately imitated and Japanized. In 645 began the period known as Hakuho, which brought the Taika reforms and saw the end of the construction of Kofun, then considered too laborious a task, as well as the rise of Buddhism among the aristocracy and the adoption of a Chinese style administration, taking the China of the Tang dynasty as its model. All over the place temples were built, and the first Shinto shrines appeared. The nobility learnt Chinese and exchanges with the Chinese mainland intensified.

In 710, at the beginning of the Tenpyo period, a new capital was built in Heijo-kyo (later to be called Nara) and the empress Gemmei ordered the compilation of provincial legends in order to put together an "official" history in 712: the *Kojiki*, "Record of Ancient Matters," revised in 720 under the name *Nihon-Shoki*. This was a time of prodigious development, both politically and culturally. New agricultural policies were put into practice and the Buddhist monasteries became increasingly powerful, laying down the law to the court. In 780 the emperor Konin decided to establish a regular army, to be in charge of the police and to conquer northern Honshu, which was then under the control of the Ainu and other barbarians. The peasants, who had up to then been free, became virtual slaves attached to monasteries or noble domains. Those who wished to escape their lot left to establish themselves in the newly conquered territories in the north, forming warrior clans to defend their lands against the barbarians. In Nara the court was sumptuous; it ordered the building of magnificent temples, consecrating an immense bronze Buddha in the Todaiji temple in 752, causing the virtual ruin of the country. Both art and literature continued to develop: this was the age of the poets of *Man'yoshu*, a famous anthology.

*Head of Buddha, from the Hakuho period
(685 A.D.). Kofuku-ji Temple, Nara.*

However, in 794 the emperor, wanting to rid himself of the tutelage of the Buddhist sects at Nara, built himself a new capital, Heian-kyo (Kyoto), which was to remain the capital of all subsequent emperors until 1868. While the conquest of the north of the country continued, and the peasant masses were held under strict subjection despite numerous agricultural reforms, the court lived a peaceful and luxurious life. In 938 official relations with the Chinese were broken off. The Japanese aristocracy from this point forward began to develop a wholly original civilization, integrating all the various elements. The splendid Heian period witnessed immense progress among the Japanese upper classes. Syllabic writing, which appeared at the beginning of the ninth century, fostered the spread of education, and women, who till then had had no access to Chinese culture, came to display a remarkable poetic imagination. Under the aristocratic and peaceable reign of the Fujiwara family, from the middle of the tenth century, Japanese civilization evolved in a wholly original manner, taking almost nothing from Korea and China. The arts flourished; palaces and temples proliferated. New Buddhist sects emerged, tending to popularize the faith through the figure of Amida, a saviour Buddha. Technology improved, and iron was better exploited. The cultivation of cotton, introduced in 799, spread, and this material began to replace silk and hemp. Mathematics progressed, but science still remained purely practical. The country was covered in monasteries, which owned immense lands and competed with the Fujiwara nobles and the State. The peasants, still very poor and burdened with taxes, hired out their labor to the monks and nobles who, to defend their own interests against those of the increasingly impoverished State, organized themselves militarily, forming warrior clans, especially in the Kanto. These clans soon clashed with each other in the struggle for supremacy and challenged the Fujiwara, now regents of the empire, for first place in the country. Two great families were to emerge above the rest, fighting each other ferociously both at court and in the provinces: they were the Taira and the Minamoto, of imperial descent.

After a bitter struggle it was the Minamoto (also called Genji) who triumphed in 1192. Their chief, Yoritomo, given the title Shogun (commander-in-chief) by the emperor, established the seat of his dictatorship at Kamakura in the Kanto, in the midst of his warriors. The Kamakura period then began. The emperor's authority grew progressively weaker, as that of the Shoguns (and later the Shikken, or regents of the Hojo family) came to exercise total control. Society became increasingly more militaristic, warriors taking precedence over the nobles. The introduction of Zen, a new Buddhist sect from China, was to give the warriors the ethical framework they were lacking. Life in Japan was conducted on almost feudal lines: the lord in authority was the Shogun, aided by his vassals (Kenin) and warriors (Samurai) who were often also peasants (Ji-samurai); the emperor was left with a purely symbolic role, as representative of the Kami in Shinto, which remained the fundamental belief of all Japanese. Buddhism was practised by most of the warriors, who at the same time adopted certain Confucian ideals. In the field of the arts painting, which had been fostered by the Fujiwara, became more popular and sculpture was realist in the extreme. Historical narrative made an appearance, replacing the romances of the Fujiwara period. New types of building appeared, to meet the needs of the new Buddhist forms of worship and of the warriors. A new culture was born, which at the same time opposed and superimposed itself on that of the aristocracy. The clans meanwhile continued to struggle against each other, and the Samurai were paid with gifts of land taken from the conquered enemy. But two Mongol attacks on north Kyushu in 1274 and 1281 threatened the established order. The entire nation joined together to repel the invaders, with the result of ruining the State financially, while saving Japan from foreign conquest. But the Samurai, who could not this time be given recompense, rebelled. Kamakura was captured by storm and set alight by a rival clan of the Minamoto, the Ashikaga, in 1333. The new Shoguns were to establish themselves in Kyoto, the better to keep an eye on the emperor and his court who had also rebelled. They made and unmade emperors. There were then two imperial courts in Japan, one in the north, one in the south, in conflict with each other, the Ashikaga supporting the one in the north. In 1392 the conflict was finally brought to an end and the Ashikaga, now all-powerful, established their own Shogunate, that of Muromachi (from the name of a district of Kyoto in which they set up their military government or Bakufu). Relations with China were resumed, the Ashikaga being avid for Chinese culture. The tea ceremony came into fashion, as did Noh theater, ceramics, paintings on mobile screens (*fusuma*) and luxurious palaces. The Ashikaga reorganized the government. But the peasant classes, reduced to greater and greater poverty, revolted, sometimes with the backing of Buddhist sects. The chief vassals of the Shogun, faced with a dispute over succession, took sides against each other. The civil war of the Onin era was to last for many years and bring ruin on the country. The town of Kyoto was utterly destroyed, the countryside laid waste. With no clan successful in gaining a decisive advantage and the Ashikaga powerless to re-establish order, the war continued to be waged in the provinces, while the imperial court, as in the past, went through the motions of governing. Innumerable little local lords, the Daimyo or "great names," declared themselves independent. Meanwhile Portuguese missionaries had landed on Kyushu and introduced fire-arms to the country. The Daimyo started building fortified castles to resist the new weapons. In effect it was anarchy that reigned supreme in the country. This state of affairs was disastrous for the peasantry, but very profitable for the merchants and craftsmen who supplied the needs of this continual war. It was then that a general emerged from the people: Oda Nobunaga who, having defeated a few other Daimyo, began to assert his authority around 1570. Helped by Hideyoshi, a valiant general, he defied one opponent after another, with the object of reuniting the country. But in 1582, betrayed by one of his own officers, he was forced to commit suicide. Hideyoshi at once stepped into his shoes and established a harsh dictatorship, aiming to force all the other Daimyo to surrender. He partially succeeded and reorganized the government. The emperor named him Kampaku, meaning Regent of the Empire. Having become all-powerful and having restored a little peace to the country, Hideyoshi then wanted to conquer Korea, in the mad ambition to ascend the throne of China. Military setbacks and his death in 1598 put an end to his aspirations. The most powerful of the Daimyo of the Kanto, Tokugawa Ieyasu, took over from Hideyoshi, having first defeated the other Daimyo leagued against him at the battle of Sekigahara in 1600. Three years later, when he had become the most powerful lord in the country, the emperor granted him the title of Shogun.

Ieyasu soon installed himself in Edo (now Tokyo) and organized his new Bakufu, continuing the work undertaken by Oda Nobunaga and Hideyoshi. He rebuilt the castle of Edo, redistributed the fiefs among his vassals, fortified Kyoto, minted money and brought the silk trade with China under control. From 1615 he laid the foundations of the new society he wished to create by promulgating his "Laws for the Military Houses" (Buke Shohatto); and, having this same year conquered the last descendants of Hideyoshi, who opposed his authority, by destroying their castle in Osaka, he firmly established his dictatorship, dividing society into distinct classes: Warriors, Cultivators, Craftsmen and Tradesmen. Under his aegis Japan extended its relations with foreign countries. One Daimyo from the north, Date Masamune, in 1613 sent a trade mission to Rome via Hawaii and Mexico. The Portuguese priests, persecuted for a time under Hideyoshi, regained a certain influence as Ieyasu wished to improve his fleet and trade with the Europeans. But the priests, accused of colluding with Spanish forces based in Manila, were soon banished again. The period of dictators Nobunaga and Hideyoshi, also known as Momoyama, witnessed a rebirth of the arts and of technology. The construction of the Daimyo castles required the co-operation of numerous artisans and traders. Artists vied with each other in decorating these castles like palaces, and the efforts put into export stimulated a growing demand for manufactured objects. Hideyoshi had brought potters from Korea who built kilns throughout the country. The arts of the tea ceremony and flower arranging flourished. The entire country rediscovered a long lost prosperity. Finally, thanks to foreign trade, the ports developed, as did the merchant navy, and the Japanese went as far as to put up godowns in south-east Asia. Although still practised by a large part of the population, Buddhism, having shown itself violently opposed to the dictators, was during this period held in check, yielding to a sort of syncretism, "Shinto-Buddhism-Confucianism," favored by the new State. The arts benefitted from the new prosperity and flourished – especially secular and anecdotal paintings – to the detriment of the "classical" schools still in vogue in court circles, and sculpture, which was virtually abandoned. Around the castles and market centers the towns expanded and prospered, thanks to the activities of artisans and merchants. The newfound peace gave cities the chance to develop and fostered the rise of a new, very rich merchant class.

On Ieyasu's death in 1616, his son and grandson Hidetada and Iemitsu carried on his work. They established a government based on the rigid division of society into classes, which were in turn divided into sub-classes. At the heart of the system a strict etiquette had to be observed, based on the social behavior of individuals who were mutually responsible for one another. The imperial court was deprived of most of its privileges, and the princely heirs had from now on to be appointed by the Shogun. Iemitsu banned Christianity and in 1638 crushed a revolt of Christian peasants at Shimabara. In 1639 he decreed that the country be closed to foreigners, but the Dutch were nevertheless allowed to continue trading from the little island of Deshima, in the port of Nagasaki. Only a few merchant ships, provided with a special permit, were authorized to leave Japanese waters to trade abroad and bring back, principally from south-east Asia, essential products such as raw silk, cotton, lead or sugar.

Throughout the entire Edo period (1603-1868) society was effectively paralyzed by the rigid structure imposed by the military Samurai caste. But though the Tokugawa Shoguns kept their most immediate vassals

Oda Nobunaga.

under firm control, some degree of autonomy was nevertheless permitted to a few important Daimyo outside, the Tozama, who owed allegiance to the Shogun of Edo only in principle. Those who rebelled were attacked and suffered the confiscation of their territories. Many Samurai in these provinces, finding themselves without a master and without work, became trouble-makers. In the by then overcrowded towns insecurity reigned and to hold on to their power the Shoguns and Samurai exercised a merciless tyranny. Any infringement of the established rules was, for the most part, punished by death. The social immobility did not however stand in the way of progress, which was particularly marked towards the end of the period. Despite much unrest, peasant revolts and periods of economic recession, due largely to the cutting back of foreign trade, artistic, literary and scientific activities continued to enhance the daily life of the Daimyo, who vied to outdo each other in elegance and luxury. In the towns a new society emerged, that of the Chonin, consisting mainly of rich traders. These men lent money to Daimyo impoverished by the costs of this life of luxury; and as, for the most part, the Daimyo were not in a position to repay the loans, they rapidly became greatly indebted to the Chonin. In this way the new class contrived to replace the Samurai, and the military government (or Bakufu) was gradually supplanted by an administration of increasingly civilian character. The Samurai managed nonetheless to maintain their prestige, though economic pressures were tending to sap the power of arms.

The Edo period, which saw the triumph of the cities (Edo, Osaka, Kyoto) and of a rich bourgeoisie, while the peasantry still lived in extreme poverty, ended in 1868 with a kind of revolution provoked by the arrival in Japanese waters of menacing European ships. The emperor's supporters, increasingly numerous, made a stand against those of the Shogunate, and after a short struggle the last of the Shoguns, Keiki, resigned his position. The young emperor Mutsuhito now took his place as ruler of the country. Installing himself in Edo, which he renamed Tokyo, he initiated a new type of government, known as *Meiji*, "enlightened government."

Under the direction of the emperor, who wished to modernize Japan and make it the equal of Western powers, the whole of Japanese society was to undergo a profound change: the Samurai lost their privileges, feudal clans were abolished, the country was redivided into prefectures placed under the authority of the central government. This government took the United States as its model and the emperor declared that all men were equal before the law. He promised to convoke an Assembly which would participate in drawing up the Constitution, to abolish all practices judged irrational, and asked everyone to participate in a world-wide search for the knowledge that Japan lacked. To bring about these ends, while easing the transition from the feudal era, he first established three classes of subjects, then he united the three into a single class of citizens of the new Empire. He also founded a national army, with the help of Prussian and French officers. Former Samurai, as would be expected, enrolled en masse, but the army also admitted men from other classes, which the Samurai found difficult to accept. One of their men, Saigo Takamori (1827-1877), rebelled at Kagoshima but, quickly overpowered by the national army, he committed suicide. The navy was reorganized on advice from British engineers and sailors, and the educational system remodelled on European lines, many foreign professors being invited to teach in the universities. Modern

The Samurai lose their privileges. *

factories were built, making armaments, paper, cement, spinning and smelting, under the direction of European engineers. The ports were modernized, railways were built from 1872, a post and telegraph service was set up, and agriculture was reorganized so as to bring uncultivated land under the plough. Japan borrowed money from London to finance part of this enormous task of modernization which under the emperor's direction was to transform the entire country within a few decades. But in order to put Japan on an equal footing with other countries, the emperor found himself obliged to adopt a more democratic form of government and, in 1890, to grant the Japanese people a Constitution. Foreign influences, particularly those of the United States and Russia, were increasingly felt and Japan, feeling its independence threatened, was to test its brand new weapons on China over its rights of sovereignty in Korea. An anti-Japanese revolt in Korea, backed by the Chinese, sparked off the conflict and in 1895 Japan declared war on China. The struggle was short-lived, the Middle Empire having but an out-of-date army with which to oppose Japan. On April 17, 1895 China was obliged to sign the treaty of Shimonoseki which gave considerable advantages to Japan, advantages which Western powers, suddenly alarmed by the success of Japanese arms, tried to minimize. Frustrated, the Japanese people embarked on a veritable arms race and, after the signing of a treaty with Great Britain, felt powerful enough to oppose Russian designs on Manchuria and Korea. Ten years after the Sino-Japanese conflict, Japan, now equipped with an ultra-modern fleet of warships, went to war with Russia, attacking Port Arthur and Vladivostok. Battles of extreme violence ensued on both land and sea. In support of his armies in the Far-East the Tsar sent his Baltic fleet, which was obliged to circumnavigate the continent of Africa to reach its destination. The Japanese were keeping watch: on May 27, 1905 admiral Togo ambushed the Russian fleet and, after a heroic battle, defeated it. The Tsar was obliged to sign the treaty of Portsmouth (USA) on September 5, 1905. Japan had proved that from now on it was the equal of Western powers. But the war effort had proved very costly and many lives had been lost. To ease its difficulties the government pursued policies alternating between the conservatives and the militarists. The economy was gradually put right and in 1910 Japan annexed Korea, despite the protests of China and the major world powers.

The Meiji emperor died in 1912 and his son Yoshihito inaugurated the Taisho era which was to last until 1926. Under Yoshihito Japan took part in the First World War and occupied German territories in the Far-East. In 1915 he imposed on a divided and powerless China his celebrated "Twenty-One Demands," which were in effect an ultimatum that established Japanese influence in China. During the Versailles peace negotiations the fates of China and Korea were not even mentioned: Japan was to be left to play a major role in the Far-East, with the tacit approval of the West.

On the death of Yoshihito in 1926 his son, Hirohito, the present emperor, took his place on the throne. The political factions in Japan engaged in bitter confrontation. Pacificists and militarists opposed each other over the question of Manchuria, which had remained unresolved. The terrible earthquake of 1923, which destroyed the city of Tokyo, proved an opportunity for industrialists to grow rich working on its reconstruction. Universal suffrage was finally adopted in 1928. Meanwhile the militarists carried the day in the government and, following a provoked "incident" in Manchuria, succeeded in taking power in 1931. The army gathered its forces, withdrew the country from the League of Nations, then invaded China. Despite uprisings in Japan the war in China continued, with the tacit agreement of Chang Kai-shek, and the Japanese troops soon confronted the Communist militia of Mao Zedong. War was formally declared against China in 1937. As the Allies were in opposition to the Japanese advance, Japan signed a tripartite pact on September 27, 1940 with Hitler's Germany and Mussolini's Italy. The only enemy still to be feared was the U.S.A. On December 7, 1941 a fleet of Japanese aircraft carriers surprised and destroyed the American Pacific fleet at Pearl Harbor in Hawaii. This was the beginning of the war in the Pacific, Japan seeking to appropriate the oil wells of south-east Asia as its own reserves could sustain its war effort for no more than six months. The Japanese armies rapidly conquered Hong Kong, Singapore, Java, the Philippines. The Japanese people, initially reluctant to accept the war, having seen the success of their armies gave their leaders wholehearted support. But America wasted no time in regathering its forces and an immense industrial effort went into rebuilding its fleet and airforce. From 1942, following the Battle of the Coral Sea on May 7, the U.S. forces began to reconquer the Pacific islands. At the Battle of Midway in the Philippines on June 4, 1942 the United States recovered their advantage and relentlessly pursued the armies of the Rising Sun, which from henceforth were fighting a losing battle. Finally, the Americans dropped two atomic bombs on Hiroshima and Nagasaki, on August 6 and 9, 1945, totally demoralizing the population. The emperor Hirohito signed the armistice on September 2, 1945.

The post-war period was fairly grim in Japan: tremendous destruction had been suffered, the number of dead was immense and the Japanese economy at zero. Moreover the country was under the control of the American administration of General MacArthur. But the Japanese people proved immensely resourceful and all harnessed their energies to the seemingly impossible task of rebuilding their country. The Korean war in 1950 was to help industry get going again, manufacturing goods essential to the American armies and others engaged in the struggle against North Korea. Japan then experienced an economic fever which brought profit to the whole nation. It rose rapidly from its own ruins and rebuilt its economy at full speed, concentrating particularly on advanced technology. Having re-established a democracy, in the space of a few years Japan made a huge leap forward, known as the "Jimmu Boom." Japan extended its security pact with the United States in 1960, was admitted to the OECD in 1963, regained the Bonin islands in 1968 and Okinawa in 1972, thus recovering its territorial integrity. From now on the conflict with the United States was to be commercial, aimed at the conquest of markets in Asia and the Pacific. Japan could now concentrate on its economic place in the world, conquering new markets from year to year. The American war in Vietnam proved a further source of profit and from then on the Japanese economy has gone from strength to strength. Thanks to the hardworking character of its people and to their mastery of the highest technological skills and knowledge, Japan has rapidly joined the ranks of the most advanced nations of the world.

Ancient Architecture

Temples and shrines

It is in the realm of religious constructions that Japanese art attains the peaks of excellence. Inhabiting a land of forests, the people of Japan have over the generations acquired great expertise in wood-carving. The first houses and the first shrines were entirely constructed of wood. After Korean Buddhism imported its temples to Japan, with their architects and tiling techniques, palaces and great temples lost their traditional thatched roofs. Powerful structures then had to be built, capable of supporting the enormous weight of roofs covered in tiles, yet flexible enough to resist, to some extent, the constant oscillations of the ground. But while Shinto shrines had pillars driven deep into the earth, the huge pillars of the new Buddhist temples, copied from analogous constructions in Korea and China, rested only on stone bases. Their one function was to hold up the roof by a complicated system of tiers of overhanging brackets and beams. Then the roofs themselves, which were set at a more-or-less up-tilted angle, also came to be constructed one above another in tiers. Walls were simple partitions placed between the pillars. From the sixth century onward a large number of buildings were constructed on this principle throughout Japan: innumerable temples, monastery gateways, various halls and pagodas (which, like the one of the Todai-ji, could rise to as many as seven storeys). The oldest dates from the beginning of the seventh century and is to be found in the Horyu-ji, south of Nara. From then on, all Japanese architecture was built on the same models, and the styles of the time were actually only methods of construction, differing from one another only in detail. Three principal methods can be distinguished: the Japanese (Wa-yo), the Chinese (Kara-yo) and the Indian (Tenjiku-yo). They differed simply in their techniques of assembly of brackets (Tokyo), the shape of pillars (straight or bulging), the arrangement of beams, the presence or absence of a stone base to pillars, the arrangement of walls, the shape of doors and windows (rectangular or curved). The only innovation was the adoption in the sixteenth century of a type of curved roof (Kara-hafu), imported from China. However if one wishes to discuss styles in Japan, it is necessary to refer not to the methods of construction but to the plans. These vary appreciably, according to the religious sect or the period.

The architecture of Shinto shrines differs markedly from Buddhist architecture. The shrines are simple rooms housing the Kami's symbolic object (generally a mirror); the faithful do not enter these rooms. Buddhist temples, on the other hand, are much bigger, having to accommodate a congregation, like Christian churches – a congregation which will be as correspondingly great in number as the

*The Kondo or main hall from the Heian
period (late eighth century). Murou-ji
Temple, Nara.*

sect is rich. The Daibutsu-den of the Todai-ji at Nara remains even today the largest wooden construction in the world. It is probable that in the Asuka period palaces were built according to the principles of Shinto architecture, the new architecture being reserved exclusively for Buddhist constructions. However the plan of the temple-monasteries became typically Japanese, comprising, as in the Horyu-ji (built at the beginning of the seventh century), a hall of worship (Hondo or Kondo) flanked by a pagoda several floors high, which was situated in the center of a great courtyard surrounded by a covered gallery broken by several doors facing north and south. In due course the plan of the temple-monasteries was modified, and the main hall was surrounded by a gallery in front of which stood two vast pagodas. A number of different arrangements existed in the Nara period, according to which the positions of doors, halls and pagodas might vary, while still observing a more-or-less symmetrical plan. Soon the temples increased in size. The hall of worship was joined by halls for sermons, libraries, belfries, refectories, dormitories for the monks, as well as annexes for a variety of uses, which progressively modified the original plans. These same plans came to be completely changed in the ninth century, with the apparition of the new esoteric sects, Shingon and Tendai, directly imported from China. The temples, situated in mountainous country and not on the plains, were built at this time to irregular plans which could adjust to the uneven terrain. Then, with the increasingly widespread adoption of the Pietist Buddhism of the sects venerating the Amida Buddha, the inner structure of the principal halls was modified. From the Fujiwara period, the statue of the deity was no longer to be found at the back of the temple, but from now on stood in the center to allow the faithful to make a ritual tour of it. The monasteries then arranged their buildings in the manner used in noble dwellings where the Shinden, or main hall, always comprised wings enclosing a garden, in which there was a pond with three little islands linked to each other and to the bank by little bridges. This tendency was accentuated by the fact that several emperors, having "retired" and become monks, built themselves residences which were palaces and monasteries at the same time. Syncretism being the fashion, the Buddhist monasteries included in their precincts little Shinto shrines, which kept their own style. In imitation of these shrines others were then built on the heights in thickly wooded spots, becoming the focal points of natural parks, whose paths were ornamented with stone lanterns and subsidiary shrines. A wall generally enclosed the precincts of the temple-monasteries, and their gateways became more and more majestic, with roofs of one or two tiers. The most remarkable is the Great Gate of the South (Nandaimon) in the Todai-ji at Nara, which was rebuilt in 1190 according to the Tenjiku-yo method (beams crossing pillars and standardization of brackets and various elements). It remains the largest gate of this type in Japan. The palaces were modelled on the Buddhist monasteries and embellished in their turn with landscape gardens, including lakes, lanterns and subsidiary pavilions. The arrival of Zen sects in Japan during the Kamakura period, under the impetus of monk Eisai in 1191, precipitated a return to Chinese plans and methods in the building of this sect's temples. Only the Kara-yo and Tenjiku-yo methods were used in their construction. At this same time the Shinto shrines developed in style: the entrance, originally set in the long wall of the hut (Shinmei style), was moved to one of the gables and the interior of the shrine was divided into two parts (Sumiyoshi and Taisha styles). Sometimes an extension was built in front of the entrance to accommodate the stairs leading to it (Taisha style). Then the plans were modified a little, sometimes adopting roofs that were curved (Kasuga style) or asymmetric (Nagare style) or joining two roofs to cover a single hall (Hachiman style). Other Shinto styles also emerged, influenced more or less by the Buddhist temples, culminating in complex structures with simple roofs which were curved and sometimes joined to each other, as in the styles known as Gion, Yatsumune, Gongen and others. Each shrine finally acquired its own individual style and could only be recognized as Shinto by the great Torii (a type of portico) leading to it, the Chigi (ornaments in the shape of horns) and Katsuo-gi (decorations on the ridge of the roof) which were characteristic. While the first Shinto shrines were extremely bare (for example those of Ise, in Shimmei style, which have been faithfully reconstructed every twenty years for over a thousand years), the later ones became increasingly ornate, like the Buddhist temples with which they on occasion became confused. The styles of the Torii themselves changed with time, though one cannot assign a precise date to each one. It was only in details that they differed from each other, their basic form remaining always the same. Nonetheless there are a few worth special notice, such as that with six pillars standing in the sea in front of the great shrine of Itsukushima.

Certain features of Buddhist architecture, the pagodas for example, are particularly remarkable. Copied from Korean and Chinese models, pagodas were generally built to a square plan and had multiple storeys (nowadays three or five roofs) of progressively decreasing size, or otherwise alternating with false storeys (west pagoda of the Yakushi-ji, near Nara), or having roofs visibly of the same size (Muroji pagoda with five roofs, Nara-ken). A type of pagoda particular to the Shingon sect is the Taho-to: on a square or octagonal base stands a sort of dome, recalling a little the Indian stupa, protected by a classic roof and crowned with a bronze ornament. In normal pagodas the last roof is often topped by a tall bronze spire with nine rings, the finishing touch to a decor of perforated bronze.

The highest pagoda in Japan is now that of To-ji, in Kyoto, which has five storeys rising over 180 feet. The majority of old pagodas have disappeared, destroyed by fires and wars, and never been rebuilt – for example those of the Todai-ji, in Nara, each of which had seven floors and was some 295 feet in height. Some remarkable examples of old pagodas are nevertheless still in existence (in the Horyu-ji and Yakushi-ji temples, and elsewhere).

The Muromachi period witnessed the development of new styles of secular architecture, designed for the pleasure of the aesthetes in power, who loved to relax in pavilions set in the midst of magnificent gardens, such as the famous gold pavilion and silver pavilion of Kyoto, and the tea pavilions which imitated simple peasant huts in costly materials and were used exclusively for the tea ceremony. The first of these Chashitsu were put up by Zen monks in the Kamakura period, but it was only from the fifteenth century that they fully developed. The Edo period saw the flowering of the palatial Shoin style, examples of which one can still admire in the Nijo castle in Kyoto. These luxurious palaces ranked with the castles built at the end of the sixteenth and beginning of the nineteenth centuries, which were initially fortresses with impressive defences and imposing dimensions, but became no more than seigniorial residences during the peace of the Tokugawa Shoguns of Edo. In the great cities of the time, the wooden houses of the townsmen gave place to dwellings made of plaster and covered in tiles, so as to limit the risks of fire.

During the Meiji period, from 1868, architecture underwent a profound transformation. The adoption of Western type building materials, bricks, cement, glass, corrugated iron, etc. led to the gradual abandonment of traditional architecture, which from now on was reserved for temples and shrines. Entire districts, as in Yokohama, were constructed in Western style and the imperial families built themselves Italian style palaces (Akasaka in Tokyo). The great earthquake of 1923 which destroyed Tokyo led to the rebuilding of the city according to new standards: wide avenues, buildings of several storeys made in concrete. This trend became even more marked in the post-war period, when sky-scrapers took over the cities. Meanwhile Japanese architects broke away from American methods and designed new structures, using the most sophisticated techniques, looking resolutely to the future (works of Tange Kenzo), or translating traditional structures into concrete, which gave rise to a wholly remarkable modern movement. Beside the work of the great architects, thousands of others built no matter what: the towns became an inextricable tangle of styles, in the absence of any overall town-planning policies. While some metropolitan districts have been entirely reconstructed (the Shinjuku district in Tokyo), in the majority of the rest thirty-storey blocks stand side by side with huts of wood and plaster.

The art of gardening, which forms an integral part of the architecture, has always been practised by the Japanese, who are exceptional horticulturalists and foresters. After the gardens of Chinese inspiration that embellished temples and palaces, new forms were brought in by Zen monks, in which water was replaced by sand and stones. These were designed to be aids to meditation, no longer merely pleasing to the eye. The Zen garden of Ryoan-ji in Kyoto is one of the best examples. The monastery paths were paved and temple parks carefully tended to give them a "natural" appearance.

One of the characteristics of Japanese architecture, regardless of style, building method and function, is its sense of space. Traditional Japanese architecture is conceived as a rational arrangement of empty space: from this comes its absence of walls, its sliding partitions, and wide openings to the outside which allow the inhabitants of the house never to be cut off from nature. The dimensions are always multiples of the *tatami*, straw mats made to the measurements of a recumbent man: a rectangle of about three feet by six, which, endlessly repeated, determines the size of rooms, the proportions of the facades, the width of the spaces between pillars. Rooms are measured in terms of single tatamis, gardens by the number of *tsubo*, meaning two tatamis. Modern buildings continue to apply the same principles. As for modern temples, which are increasingly numerous in Japan, they are hybrid monuments, combinations of concrete and traditional forms, imitating a Chinese door here, a railway station there. However the steel and concrete walls are clad in wood and the roof, while covered in tiles (or even thatch), is supported by a solid layer of concrete, against fire and earth tremors. Modern temples serve at the same time as schools, universities, sports grounds, libraries, meeting and prayer places. Because, in what we understand by the name religion, the Japanese are decidedly unable to separate the sacred from the profane.

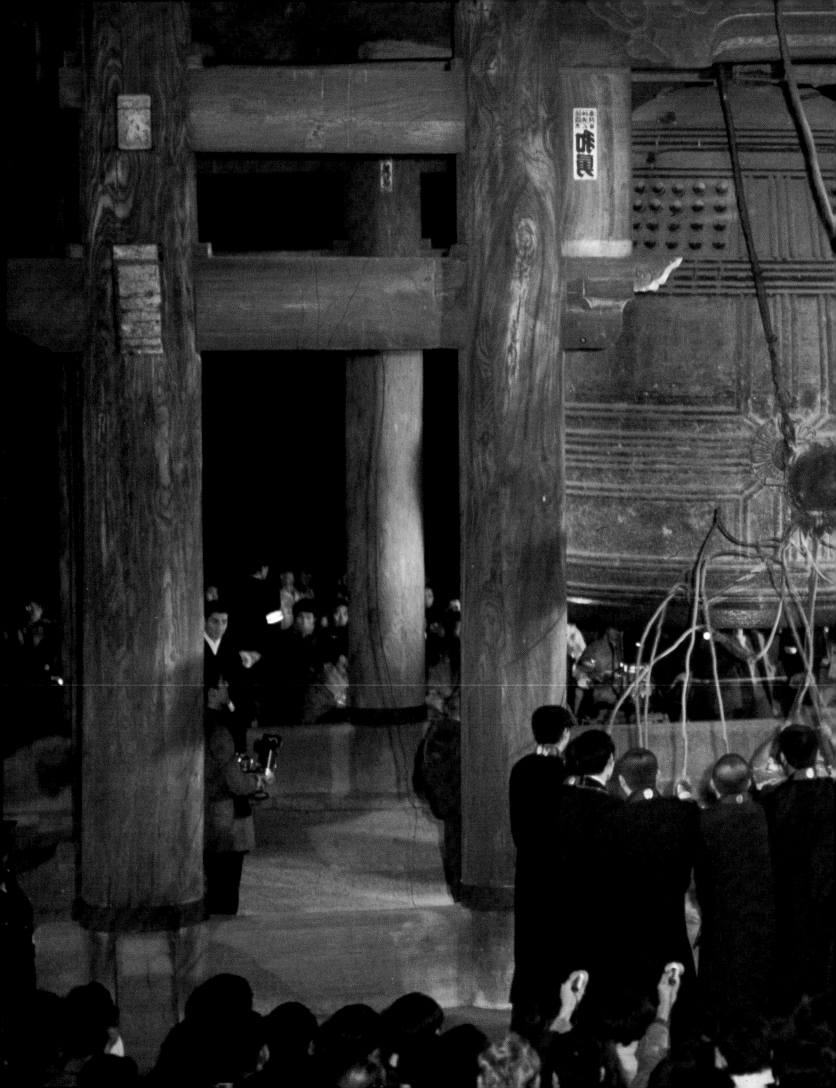

44

44. TOSHOGU SHRINE in the Nikko district. When the emperor Tokugawa Ieyasu died he was given divine status. This shrine was built and he was worshipped as Toshogu Daigongen, his cult centered on Nikko and Sumpu. He was deified not for his personal qualities but in recognition of his role as protector of the social and political order that he had established during his lifetime. This deification of historical figures revived an ancient religious practice that proved to be a unifying force in Japanese life. The temple, in the ornate Ming style, was constructed in 1652.

45. Cherry blossoms and a small castle: symbols of Japan.

46

46. *ASAKUSA, Tokyo. This Buddhist temple was one of the most frequented religious buildings in the Edo period and remains so today.*

47. *OGAMIO (prayer).*

48. *HOZEN-JI. Buddhist temple in Osaka.*

47

48

50

49. *HEIAN SHRINE, Kyoto. Washing hands and mouth before prayer for purification.*

50. *DAI-BUTSU. The Great Buddha in Kamakura. When Buddhism first came to Japan, there was little attempt to convert the bulk of the people who remained Shinto. However, when Kyoto became the capital, during the Heian period (800 to 1185 A.D.), Buddhism began to permeate all levels of society and to spread through the land.*

51

51-53. *HI-NO MATSURI in the village of Kurama. A famous fire festival held near Kyoto on October 22nd. Along with water, fire is held to be the most efficacious method of purification. From 5,30 p.m. hundreds of young people carry burning torches to the shrine. The festival continues until late at night.*

52

54. TODAIJI TEMPLE, Nara. Home of the Great Buddha. This is the greatest construction in wood in the entire world, measuring 51 meters in height. Founded in 752, the temple has suffered severe damages in the past but it has always been carefully reconstructed.

55. HASEDERA TEMPLE, Nara. Nara was the ancient capital of Japan, founded in 710 at the start of the Tenpyo period. It was then known as Heijo-kyo.

56. KASUGA SHRINE, Nara.

54

55

57. NIGATSU-DO TEMPLE, *Nara. Deer in the snow. During the Nara period, Nara itself was a Buddhist center, there being seven monasteries in or near the city. The ecclesiastical property attached to the monasteries paid no taxes and peasants at the time were quite willing to surrender their lands to the church in order to hold it as tenants at a rent far lower than the taxes levied by the government. Under this system monastery holdings increased at a rapid pace.*

57

58

59

60

58. *A traditional Japanese house. Wood is the primary material for building as Japan has an abundant supply of excellent timber. The houses are low, one or at most two storeys, and the roofs are made of grey tiles, or in the country, of thatch. The house is divided into rooms by a series of sliding panels which can be removed to turn several rooms into one large one. On the floor are closely-fitted mats about two inches thick. At night the house is closely shuttered by wooden panels running in grooves on the outside.*

59. *JIZO, in stone. One of the most popular deities belonging to Mahayana Buddhism, Jizo is the guardian of children. Mahayana or "the great vehicle" was a newer, more elaborate form of Buddhism than the earlier Hinayana and became popular in Japan in the Nara period.*

60. *Buddhist monks praying in a temple.*

Beliefs and Traditions

Myths, religions and cults

Very little is known of the primitive beliefs of the Japanese people before the introduction of Buddhism around 538 A.D. It is probable, however, that they were animistic in character and that all natural phenomena, mountains, trees, rocks, rivers, were personified in a sort of superior spirit (Kami) which represented Nature in its entirety. There undoubtedly existed an anthropomorphic conception of the gods, as evidenced by the myths and legends recorded in provincial chronicles and the "historical" records compiled at the beginning of the eighth century. However, neither the Kami nor their powers were precisely defined. There are no indications of metaphysical speculation. Every deceased person became a Kami and each one of these divinities could manifest itself on earth by temporarily inhabiting an object, a tree, a rock, and so on. The only prescribed rite was that of purification by water (*misogi*) which took place primarily after contact with death. The shamans, sorcerers and soothsayers were at the time often women. Later, however, the clan chiefs arrogated to themselves religious powers, which consisted above all in invocations (*norito*), ritual dances (*kagura*) and worship of ancestors. It is this religious function that the emperors of Japan have handed down to each other over the centuries. Their power was symbolized by three objects, a mirror, a sword and jewels, each of which represented a spiritual sphere: the mirror representing the divinity of the Kami, the sword, temporal power, the jewels (*magatama*), wealth. With the strengthening of central authority, it was the myths and legends of the most important clan, that of Yamato, which came to predominate. According to this mythology, the Japanese islands were created by a brother-sister couple, Izanagi and Izanami, who descended from "the high plain of the sky" and gave birth to the great celestial Kami, one of whom was Amaterasu, the sun goddess, from whom the first rulers of Yamato are descended. An entire pantheon of Kami soon surrounded Amaterasu, and there were numerous legends to explain the birth of the other Kami, of the stars – indeed everything to be found on earth. During the course of the fourth, fifth and sixth centuries the ideas of Taoism and Confucianism came to the islands from the continent and were adapted to the Japanese cast of mind, in which they inculcated certain ethical ideas. But nothing was codified, and this varied collection of beliefs only came to be called Shinto, "Way of the Kami," to distinguish it from Buddhism (Bukkyo), when the latter was adopted by the court. Initially a fierce rivalry existed between the Shinto and Buddhist clans, but more over the question of political pre-eminence than for religious reasons. Though Buddhism won the favor of the aristocracy, Shinto nonetheless

61. Pilgrim, near Kyoto.

continued as the original belief of Japan. The Japanese were from then on Shinto and Buddhist at the same time, at any rate in the court, Shinto remaining the only religion of the people. Under the influence of Buddhism, Shinto began to organize itself. Its shrines, simple wooden huts housing symbolical objects, grew more and more elaborate, keeping up with the architectural norms in existence well before the arrival of the new religion.

Buddhism came to Japan from Korea and was officially established in Japan towards the middle of the sixth century, to be definitively adopted by prince Shotoku in 604. Throughout the Asuka period (592-628) the heads of the great families of Japan were firm supporters of Buddhism and participated in the construction of numerous temples modelled on those in Korea. Buddhist monks traveled to China at this time in order to bring back various texts and teachings, which came to have a lasting influence on the Japanese state in its infancy. During the Nara period Buddhism developed considerably: six sects established themselves in this capital and shortly came to dominate spiritual, political and social life. In 655 there was an order that each house put up a little altar to the Buddha (*Butsudan*), on the same lines as the altar dedicated to the Kami (*Kamidana*). During the Taika reforms, however, Shinto was not overlooked and a sort of ministry, the Jingi-kan, was given the task of administering its shrines, while the emperor, although a Buddhist, remained the supreme Shinto priest. The six Nara sects (Sanron, Jojitsu, Hosso, Kusha, Kegon and Ritsu) all emerged between 625 and 734 and became so powerful, their monasteries owning so much land, that the emperor grew uneasy and decided to build himself a new capital, Heian-kyo, away from the direct influence of the monks. Then he despatched two monks to China. Their names were Saicho and Kukai, and their task was to bring back new and more suitable doctrines in which salvation was not reserved exclusively for monks but was accessible to common mortals. The two sects of Chinese origin which the monks brought back with them were Shingon (the True Word) and Tendai (after mount Tiantai in China). Saicho's Tendai sect, established on mount Hiei near Kyoto, assimilated the Shinto Kami to the Buddhist divinities in a move to popularize belief in the Buddha. As for Kukai, he claimed that the Shinto Kami were incarnations of the Buddhist divinities; he identified Amaterasu with a supreme, solar, Buddha and called this syncretic religion Ryobu-Shinto. Soon Buddhist monks took charge of the Shinto shrines and Shinto priests participated in Buddhist ceremonies. The faithful became rapidly incapable of distinguishing between the two religio§s. Yet the celebration of all happy occasions was reserved for Shinto, while funeral ceremonies were left to Buddhism, the monks from now on being regarded as unclean. Everyone practised ancestor worship. The esoteric doctrines of the Shingon and Tendai sects, however, remained difficult to understand and the people barely grasped them. It was at this point that a new sect appeared, that of Amida, whose Pietist character demanded no effort of comprehension, but only absolute faith in the total mercy of the Amida Buddha. The sect excited immediate and universal interest in all circles of society. People saw it as an easy way of ensuring a "good death" and happy reincarnation. This sect, Jodo, "Pure land" of Amida (the name given to paradise), spread rapidly in the countryside, where Buddhism had as yet scarcely penetrated, thanks to missionaries who opened schools and danced and sang the name of the Amida Buddha with the villagers. New types of temples were built, new rites and ceremonies developed, both the nobility and the common people taking part. Honen (1132-1212), a defector from Tendai, directed the sect as if it were independent and proclaimed that the mere recitation of the name of Buddha was enough to guarantee salvation. Faced with the increasing popularity of this new faith, the monks of other sects joined forces to suppress it and, winning the emperor over to their cause, had Honen driven out of Kyoto in 1207. But the Amida cult had attracted too powerful a following and Honen was restored to the favor of the court one year before his death. One of his disciples, Shinran (1173-1262), also a defector from Tendai, founded a new form of Amidism which he called Jodo Shin (sect of the true pure land); he also had a family, contrary to the customs of the Buddhist monks, who took vows of celibacy. Other Amidist sects then sprang up, differing little in doctrine from one to another: the Yuzu Nembutsu preached, like the adherents of the Kegon sect, that there existed perfect oneness among all beings and things in the universe, all having a share in the same Unicity. The Ji sect, founded by Ippen (1239-1289), asserted that when one repeated the Nenbutsu, meaning invocation, "there exists no more of Self, nor even of Buddha, but only the invocation," and put emphasis on trance-like dances. All sects and sub-sects tended to popularize Buddhism. They succeeded to a very great extent and inculcated certain fundamental ideas in the minds of the Japanese people, such as the impermanence of all things, the certainty of finding welcome, after death, in the paradise of Amida and of achieving a "good death."

At the end of the twelfth century the doctrines of the Chinese Chan sect, already known in Japan during the Nara period and included in the teaching of Tendai, were revived by the monk Tendai Eisai (1141-1215) when he returned from a second voyage to China in 1191. He founded at Kyoto the Rinzai sect of Zen (the Chinese Chan) and a little later transferred his headquarters to Kamakura, as he was in favor with the Shoguns. Not long after, a monk Dogen (1200-1253) founded another Zen sect which he called Soto. The object of Zen was directly to transmit the spirit of Buddha to that of believers. To achieve this the accent was laid on the total purity of the spirit, only to be attained by meditating on the emptiness of all things. Illumination (called Satori) could only come by intuitive thought. There was no longer a place for it in Zen, in the sacred formula, in the belief in whatever saviour, in the veneration of deities, but only in a personal effort intuitively to understand the Reality of the universe by means of an aesthetic perception of Reality. The only difference between the two branches of Zen was that one saw the illumination as a sudden phenomenon, and the other as a gradual phenomenon. "Special transmission outside the Scriptures; no reliance on words and letters; direct aim at man's soul; examination of his own nature; and a reaching for the nature of Buddha," such is the major teaching of Zen. This religion, more of a philosophy, was however still too abstract for ordinary mortals, who preferred Pietist doctrines. But its quality of detachment from all finality, of Impermanence, found favor among the warriors, who adopted it with enthusiasm. The Zen monks had brought from China certain Confucian philosophies, such as those formulated by Zhuxi in the twelfth century. Little by little these Confucian doctrines overtook the Buddhist ones and finally came to constitute the ethical basis of the feudal government of Edo. Pure Zen diminished in importance, despite the fact that a new branch of this belief, Obaku, had been imported from China by the Chinese monk Ingen (1592-1673). This branch of Zen accepted the Buddhist scriptures, among them the Amida Sutra.

The Zen sects, and the spirit which they instilled in the nobility, inspired the revival of Chinese studies at the time of the Ashikaga Shoguns, as well as the aesthetic sense. The arts of Noh, the tea ceremony and flower arranging (Ikebana) owe their origins very largely to Zen. There was in fact a fairly clear distinction between Zen and Chinese Chan, in that Zen was a blend of Buddhist ideas and Shinto. The latter contributed the innate feeling for nature that the Japanese showed from their earliest beginnings, as well as an aesthetic sense recalling to some degree that of the aristocracy in the Fujiwara period. Zen's success came from the fact that it perfectly reflected the Japanese cast of mind, which inclined both to Shinto beliefs and to Buddhism. But Zen had a serious rival from the very moment it began to develop. In the thirteenth century a Tendai monk, Nichiren (1222-1282), founded a new sect with the object of unifying the other Buddhist sects, which in his view derived from perversions of the primitive teaching of Sakyamuni Buddha. As the object of his veneration, its study alone being valid, he took the Lotus Sutra, an Indian text dating from about the time of Christ. He wanted to reform Buddhism and restore its true raison d'être, so began from then to criticize existing sects and in particular the Amidist sects. Accused of heresy and of rebellion (because he prophesied that the Shoguns of Kamakura would suffer terrible disasters if they did not reform their beliefs), he was banished in 1261, then again in 1264. But on his return to Kamakura in 1272 he continued to preach, seeing himself as the savior of the country. Fanatical in the extreme, he transformed his version of Buddhism into a political movement which the leaders of the time were forced to reckon with. In 1274, the same year in which the Mongols launched their first attack on the Japanese coast, he retired to Minobu on the slopes of mount Fuji.

He died after the second attempted Mongol invasion, in 1282, not far from Tokyo. Nichirenism, tough rejected by the Samurai, was well received by the people and also by the nobility of Kyoto, who saw it as a means of taking revenge on the military. The confrontation between the followers of the various Buddhist sects and the Nichirenites occasionally grew violent, and the monks came to the point of armed battle. Despite the fact that they were compelled to silence during the Tokugawa period, Nichiren's followers continued to grow in number, their fierce nationalist spirit finding favor with the bourgeoisie. The adherents of the Nichiren doctrines remain very influential to this day, working in various lay and religious organizations, such as the Soka Gakkai. During the Edo period, the Confucian doctrines adopted by the Shoguns and some of the Samurai relegated to the shadows the majority of Buddhist sects, which no longer drew a following except among the poorer people. In the countryside, which remained impervious to the intellectualism of Nichiren, it was the Amida sects which predominated.

When in 1459 Francis Xavier landed in Japan, Christianity was virtually unknown. At first the Japanese largely regarded it as a form of Buddhism. Many were converted, following the example of their lords, above all on Kyushu Island, and it is estimated that around the year 1600 Christians numbered several hundreds of thousands. Initially the Buddhists tolerated the intrusion of this foreign doctrine, but when

Christianity showed itself to be intolerant, they opposed it fiercely. The dissension among the Christian sects, the allegiance to Rome of the Catholic priests from Spain and Portugal, made the authorities uneasy. In 1587 Christianity was forbidden and its priests banished. Hideyoshi ordered the persecution of missionaries who had gone into hiding and continued to make conversions: twenty-six of them were crucified in Nagasaki in 1597. The persecutions continued until, in 1639, Japan cut itself off from the rest of the world at the bidding of the Shoguns. Only the Dutch, not being suspected of proselytizing, were permitted to remain on the island of Deshima, near Nagasaki.

Throughout the Edo period, despite the fact that it was the religion recognized by the State, Buddhism was in constant decline, except perhaps for the Amidist sects, whose followers were not suspected of nursing political thoughts hostile to the government. Shinto came back to the fore with the revival of the study of history and the Mito school of historians, which published numerous studies on the *Nihongi* and preached a return to the "national" divinities, taking the view that Buddhism and Christianity were beliefs alien to the true spirit of Japan. There followed a form of official disaffection from Buddhism, which suffered the closing of many of its temples, while monks were reduced to poverty. On the other hand there was a blossoming among the general populace of new sects of Shinto inspiration and the government moved towards making Shinto a type of official religion. This tendency became more marked as the autority of the Shogunate weakened and the supporters of the emperor grew more active, wishing to see the traditional head of Shinto return to power.

In 1868 the emperor was restored to his place at the head of the government, and Shinto was officially separated from Buddhism in 1882, after a vain attempt to establish a national religion amalgamating Buddhism and Shinto. The ban on Christianity was lifted in 1873 under pressure from foreign countries. Shinto, now promoted to national religion and official form of worship, was divided into "Shinto of the shrines" and "Shinto of the sects," so as to make a clear differentiation between the State doctrines and those of the new sects. While total religious freedom was permitted in Japan, the State insisted on the "Japanese" virtues of Shinto and, in his "Rescript on Education" dated 1890, the Meiji emperor commended loyalty to the emperor and respect for the "Way of the Kami." The move was to establish a truly national religion under the direction of the emperor in his capacity of high-priest of the country.

In the decade leading up to the Second World War, the State Shinto became virtually identified with nationalism and growing militarism. Buddhism, not wishing to isolate itself from the future of the nation, fell into step, as moreover did most of the Christian churches. Throughout the war religion was completely at the service of the State. Every day special prayers were said at the Shinto shrine of Yasukini in Tokyo for the victory of the Japanese armies. Monks and priests who refused to collaborate with the war effort were imprisoned. The three main religions of Japan, Shinto, Buddhism and Christianity, were at the time brought together in a single "Religious and patriotic association of Great Japan at war," under the direction of the ministry of education. After the end of the war this organization became a religious League, the three religions co-operating to help bring about the moral recovery of the country. But soon each went its separate way. Today Buddhism has regained much of its former dominance, in particular the Amida and Nichiren sects, while Shinto is still tacitly practised by all and sundry, more as a custom than as a true religion. Shinto does not in fact promulgate any dogma or philosophy: it is no more than a collection of rites of worship of the ill-defined deities known as Kami. As for Christianity, it still has a fairly strong influence, particularly in the big cities. Outside the main religions there are also numerous independent sects, not properly owing allegiance to any religion, but commanding a great following all the same, for example the Tenri-kyo, Seicho no Ie and Sumera-Kyo sects. Muslims make up only a tiny minority of the population, with less than a thousand believers. Many Japanese claim to have no particular religious belief. They continue nonetheless to practise the Shinto rites and to turn to Buddhism when it comes to burials. Because if Shinto remains in the Japanese mind the symbol of life, Buddhism is still the symbol of death and the uncertainties of the after-life in the Great Beyond. Religion has become a sort of comprehensive insurance policy.

Customs, traditions, feasts

There are innumerable customs in Japan and a great many of them are observed in everyday life and social activities. For the Japanese this perpetuation of tradition is a way of preserving their identity in a world of ceaseless change moving towards uniformity of life style and of thought. Japanese society, in its state of perpetual evolution, has had to abandon, above all since the Second World War, a number of customs which no longer correspond to modern life styles. This is particularly true of the Japanese style of dress, now increasingly Westernized. Nonetheless many customs or ways of being and behaving have been jealously preserved, like family treasures handed down from father to son. The Japanese language is perhaps the first and most important of these customs, as it is the means of perpetuating certain ideas, certain concepts not found in other countries. Although the Japanese language has never been properly codified, it is constantly evolving, both in its vocabulary and its syntax, sometimes so rapidly that a young man nowadays would have difficulty understanding his great-grandfather if the latter were to address him in pre-war Japanese. New words have been taken over from foreign languages, American English in particular, and given Japanese pronunciations. New expressions have been added to a basic vocabulary of very ancient origins, including forms of words derived from a variety of linguistic sources. While in the West we have had an educated language, which is written, and popular spoken languages, the Japanese have in the course of history evolved different forms of speech according to social class or even according to sex: a Samurai does not express himself in the same way as a peasant, and a woman uses particular phrases indicating her social position. Similarly the way in which someone refers to himself or addresses another person depends on their relative positions. Nowadays the Japanese language is tending towards uniformity and models itself on what is spoken in Tokyo, the capital. However, there are marked differences between the dialects spoken in the provinces and a person from Tokyo may experience a certain difficulty understanding an inhabitant of Kyoto or Nagasaki. To this day women use verbs or forms of speech which would never be spoken by a man. A foreign man who happened to have learned the language through contact with women would be laughed at for speaking "makura-nihongo," meaning pillow talk. On the same principle, soldiers tend to speak a rough language which would be considered very rude on the part of a civilian. In conversation one hesitates to mention by name or personally refer to the person one is speaking to or about: not because there are no personal pronouns in Japanese, but because it is considered unbecoming to use them often. When someone joins a conversation half-way through, it can sometimes prove difficult to discover the identity of the person under discussion. This shows the persisting influence on the language of feudal customs, which dictated that relations between individuals be governed by a strict hierarchy. The Japanese language is thus a storehouse of archaisms bequeathed by the past, polite formulas essential in a country which is subject to the pressures of a dense population, in practice a syntax which seems strange to us because it corresponds to ways of thinking that are not ours.

It is impolite brutally to contradict someone, or to answer no to a question, because one might cause the person to whom one is talking to lose face. So one uses circumlocutions. Instead of telling someone that they are wrong or have made a mistake, one says that one is of a different opinion, which saves the other person's feelings. Phrases are constructed on different principles to ours; as there is no article, the function of each component of a phrase must be indicated by an enclitic, a little word which makes each function clear (subject, genitive, locative, vocative, etc.) and the active verb is always tossed in at the end. When it comes to numbers, the way one counts is determined by what one is counting (animals, birds, human beings), depending on its shape (long, flat, etc.) or subject (days, months, for example). The Japanese language took over a number of Chinese terms, as a result of which there were two main ways of counting, the Sino-Japanese and the Yamato (i.e. truly Japanese), and these two combined. Moreover Japanese words (Yamato being a polysyllabic language) constantly mingle with words taken from Chinese, which is monosyllabic. The same Sino-Japanese ideographic character can be read in the Yamato way or in several "Chinese" ways, depending on when the word was introduced or where it came from, without there being any very precise rules: it is all a matter of custom. Buddhist monks do not pronounce words in the same way as lay people. Another point, the Japanese language being extremely poor in sounds (66 simple sounds and 36 "compound" ones), homophones are extraordinarily numerous. This has given rise to curious superstitions, such as that which makes four an unlucky number because its sound, Shi, also means death. For similar reasons other numbers are also considered unlucky: 42 (Shi-ni, also meaning death) and 33 (San-zan, also meaning ruthless). On the other hand the numbers 77 and 88 are considered auspicious, respectively meaning happy and rice.

Politeness requires that everything belonging to the person who is speaking be gently deprecated (house, wife, children, objects), while anything to do with the person spoken to should be praised, and often introduced by an honorary prefix (O- or, go-). This honor is also accorded to objects regarded as traditional and worthy of respect, even if they do not belong to anybody in particular, as for example the traditional bath, O-furo. For all this, with the pressures of life in the age of technology, polite formulas and elaborate turns of phrase are gradually fading out. The young in Japan tend to adopt an over-simplified, at times even uncouth form of speech, turning up their noses at particles and other affectations of the polite language, to the great regret of the purists.

But language, though it may be the first and most important of the Japanese customs, is not the only one. Japanese customs could in fact be classified into distinct categories in the Western manner: customs in the context of religion, of social relations, of nature, of history, and so on. But this would not be compatible with the Japanese way of thinking, which does not separate things nor set them in opposition, but prefers rather to superimpose them on each other. The Japanese themselves show little concern with classification, preferring to follow the course of time, the natural cycle in all its forms being intimately bound up with the development of the social and thinking animal that is man. The customs of the Japanese are more habits than rules and no one is obliged to observe them in order to comply with moral or other prescriptions. Morality, in the sense in which the West knows it, does not exist in Japan; there are only unspoken rules of behavior, and religion is more a matter of superstitions and rites than of profound faith. It is important to respect certain rules, to know how to live in society, rather than to live up to any moral principles. If there is a morality, it can only be Confucian (teaching the obedience of son to father and man to the family and the State) or Buddhist (teaching compassion), since Shinto only has a conception of what is pure and impure. Morality is a question for the individual, not the group.

Customs, when they are not religious or superstitious, nearly always concern the relationship of individuals to each other and to the natural world. It is of utmost importance not to lose face, yet this is not a question of pride but of personal dignity. This obliges the Japanese to respect the consensus of opinion and observe customs because their fathers did so, for it would be unseemly in the eyes of their compatriots and themselves not to conform. So people observe customs and feasts, celebrate historical events, without ever separating these from everyday life, itself organized in rhythm with the seasons.

The first of the great annual feast days is New Year's Day (O-Shogatsu), which merges into that of the last day (Omisoka): this is a time of celebration and good cheer, the feast of life's renewal. Special dishes are prepared as the first month is supposed to be lived lavishly, to set an example for the rest of the year. As the Japanese are gourmets no feast day goes by without a celebratory meal. Some foods are auspicious, such as sea bream (Tai), sweet potatoes and Daikon (a type of large radish), and a great deal of them is eaten, to the accompaniment of Sake, a rice wine (16°-18° proof) which is drunk warm. At the beginning of the year it is the custom to visit one's family and friends and to write poems. People also visit temples and shrines, returning with charms which will bring them luck throughout the year. Another custom, this time of American origin, is to send greetings cards which portray the animal of that year according to the Chinese calendar (rat, ox, tiger, rabbit, dragon, snake, horse, sheep, monkey, cock, dog and wild boar). The year 1986 for example is the Year of the Tiger. The Japanese, being highly superstitious, take astrology very seriously and on all kinds of occasions they consult the almanac or an astrologer or fortune-teller; if the day is supposedly unpropitious they will not embark on anything. Putting the harshness of the weather to advantage as a way of toughening oneself up, it is also customary to practise martial or other arts. Then one visits the shrine of Ebisu, one of the seven gods of good fortune, to pay him homage and obtain good luck. January 6 is the date of the firemen's feast in Tokyo, which draws enormous crowds: fires are greatly dreaded in Japan. Every day in the month of January is the occasion of a particular celebration, varying from region to region. The entire country, however, eagerly looks forward to the "change of season" (Setsubun) which occurs on February 3 or 4 of our calendar and in former times marked the beginning of spring. This is the moment to get rid of demons, chasing them away by throwing soya beans. Everyone takes part in this public ceremony, politicians, actors, celebrities and children. Analogous ceremonies are held in the temples, varying according to the sect. On this same day, February 4, people also celebrate the courage of the "47 Ronin," or Samurai without masters: in 1701 they avenged their master who had been made to lose face by a noble lord in the court of the Shogun. Their vengeance wrought, they all committed suicide together. Inari, the Kami of cereals, is also feted, in the interest of obtaining good harvests. In Hokkaido at this time of year competitions of ice statues are staged. Ceremonies and celebrations succeed one another almost without break, from the beginning of the year to the end. The majority of them are local, and the same occasions may be celebrated at different dates in different regions.

One day universally celebrated in Japan is the feast of dolls, falling on the third day of the third month, in other words March 3. Little girls put out a series of little figures representing the imperial court in olden times and make the most of the day by inviting their friends and putting on their best clothes.

From the beginning of April the cherry trees begin to flower. Everyone hastens to admire them as the fragile blossoms do not last very long. Cherry blossom symbolizes the soul of Japan: its delicacy, its hesitant color and the briefness of its passage symbolize for the Japanese the fragility and transience of their own lives. Families and friends gather under the cherry trees, singing, dancing, eating a great deal and drinking even more: life is so fleeting, like the flowering of the cherry, that one must hasten to make the most of it. Buddhists celebrate the anniversary of the birth of Buddha (April 8); women's groups celebrate their attainment of equality with men; the people of Nagasaki admire the huge kites that men send soaring up into the heavens.

On April 11 comes the anniversary of the death of prince Shotoku Taishi: various Shinto and Buddhist festivals then take place. In Kyoto the textile artisans hold their annual festival. All the towns are decorated with plastic cherry branches which light up. Then comes the time of the first baseball matches. This American game was brought in at the end of the last century and adopted with delirious enthusiasm by the young. In Nagasaki processions and boat races are held in celebration of the opening of the port to foreign trade in the sixteenth century. The Japanese delight in historical reconstructions in period dress. At festival time they frequently stage processions representing members of the court of the emperor or Shogun, riding on horses; in chariots, escorted by Samurai, winding their way down the city streets, standards waving in the wind, carving a path with difficulty through the crowds of spectators, amidst the traffic and people in their Sunday best. A curious juxtaposition, historic Japan advancing down the streets of ultra-modern cities.

The fifth day of the fifth month, namely May 5, is the feast of boys (Tango no Sekku). Each family proudly erects a pole on the roof of their house, to which are attached, floating in the wind, as many multi-colored carps as there male children. Little boys are given copies of Samurai armor. They are kings for the day and their every whim is indulged. It goes without saying that special food is prepared and people get together to celebrate. Because the Japanese, though they often appear stiff and formal, in reality love to live life to the full and never miss an occasion to enjoy themselves. And how else to do this if not at meals with one's friends?

Children are particularly spoilt in Japan and, up to the age of four, are allowed to do exactly what they please. A few days after birth they are taken to the temple or shrine to receive the gods' blessing, and again at the ages of 3, 5 and 7, each visit being an occasion for rejoicing and a chance to put on one's best kimono. After the age of four they go to school and their training in communal life begins. From then on their parents are stricter and begin to teach them good manners by example.

The second Sunday in May is Mother's Day, a Western feast day that Japan has adopted. The whole of this month is given over to feasts and religious or historic celebrations. The most important event of the month is the great historic procession in Kyoto, Aoi Matsuri, which is generally held on the 15th. On this occasion hundreds of men and women in period dress parade down the streets of this former capital, re-enacting the vicissitudes of the emperor's pilgrimages in the Heian period. The ceremonials and rites of the time are scrupulously respected and huge crowds throng the streets marveling at the splendors of the procession. A few days later in Kyoto productions of Noh theater are staged in the open air, and last for hours.

Next comes June, which is the rainy month (Baiu or Tsuyu). This is the time when the mistress of the house habitually does her spring cleaning and both husband and children had best keep out from underfoot. Clothes and objects have to be protected from damp. This is also the time for transplanting the young rice shoots and in the country no work gets under way or finishes without song, dance and merriment. Although it rains heavily throughout June this in no way stops festivals taking place: the most famous is the great race of dragon-boats at Nagasaki, commemorating an old Chinese legend.

Summer is the season of the iris, whose leaves are shaped like the blades of swords. The great festival of the Atsuta shrine in Nagoya is held at the beginning of the summer, in honor of the sacred sword that is preserved there. The 1st of July is the official opening of the climbing season on mount Fuji (which in former days was forbidden territory to women). On the 7th is the feast of stars (Tanabata), celebrated throughout the country, and bringing to mind the old Chinese legend which tells of the mythical union of Vega (the weaver) and the Wagoner beyond the Milky Way. Young Japanese pray to the stars to bring them luck in love. In schools, the children dance and sing songs specially written for the occasion, and the municipalities decorate the streets with cascades of colored ribbons. In the countryside people feast, make merry and down plenty of Sake. Then comes the 15th of July, great feast of souls, O-Bon, which usually lasts for seven days: a bowl is laid on the table for the soul of a dear departed one who is supposed to pay a visit on this day. Also known as the feast of lanterns, O-Bon is observed by everyone, despite its Buddhist origins. People visit cemeteries where urns containing the ashes of the dead are interred, for the burial of bodies has been a rare practice since the seventh century. On the last day little boats bearing flowers and a candle are launched on the waters of a river: they are supposed to carry the souls of the departed to the land of the dead. Rituals vary from family to family and region to region, but are always faithfully carried out. The school summer holidays then begin and are divided up between trips across country in cheerful school parties and visits to famous sites in busloads. Parents are not in the habit of taking holidays and, although entitled to a few days off, they generally prefer to take them in bits and pieces. Japan is unacquainted with the general exodus that marks the start of the summer holidays in many Western countries. In mid-July the festival of Gion takes place in Kyoto, with a procession of immense wagons surmounted by a type of high peak symbolizing a mountain. Meanwhile in Osaka it is the feast of the minister Sugawara Michizane who was exiled in Kyushu in 903 and afterwards became the god of literature.

The end of summer, which occurs at the beginning of August, coincides with the last of the great heat waves: clothes are aired and it is time for another great cleaning session. Festivals follow each other in quick succession: it is the turn of the town of Sendai, in the north, to celebrate Tanabata, one month later than elsewhere. In the neighboring city of Akita the festival of lanterns is held and men bear on their shoulders lanterns of fantastical construction. On August 15, the St. John's day of Japan, temples are ablaze with thousands of lanterns and, on a mountain close to Kyoto, a huge fire is lit in the form of the Sino-Japanese character meaning "great," while fireworks shoot in all directions. In Tokushima it is now the feast of Awa at which the country people wear regional dress, sing and dance for three days, accompanied by spectators.

Autumn is the time of year for marriages, at which, in the presence of a Shinto priest or the assembled family, the betrothed couple make a ritual exchange of three cups of Sake which they drink in three goes (Sansankudo) to seal their union. Traditional marriages in a Shinto shrine still take place, but they are usually now accompanied by a great ceremonial banquet in a hotel or restaurant specializing in such functions, at which the most unbridled of fantasies can be indulged. The marriage has no religious function, but only a social one: its purpose is to let everyone know that two families, in the persons of the bridal couple, have been united. Ridiculous sums are spent on the occasion and the guests, who have had their presents, often of cash, delivered before the ceremony, are at the end of the meal given a small gift of food in acknowledgement. The banquet often ends in the absence of the newly weds, who have discreetly slipped away before its conclusion. Autumn is the most propitious time to travel in Japan and go on the traditional pilgrimages, whether one is a believer or not: they provide yet another occasion to get together and have fun. In mid-September one goes out to contemplate the full moon and recite poems while feeding on round cakes (O-dango). October and November take their courses, punctuated by a variety of festivals. One of the most famous is held at the end of October in Kyoto, the Jidai Matsuri or "festival of a bygone age." A great procession of historic figures, wearing the costumes of the Heian period, recall to mind the transfer of the capital in 794 from Nara to Heian-kyo. The month of November is dedicated to culture: the treasures of the Shoso-in Museum in Nara are brought out and all children aged 3, 5 or 7 (Shichigosan) are fêted. Exhibitions of chrysanthemums and works of art are held everywhere, as are tea ceremonies and artistic and literary shows. People visit gardens and craft workshops and practise calligraphy. The month is quickly over and December is a crucial time as custom has it that all debts should be paid before the year is out. In preparation for Christmas (in Japan a children's feast of purely commercial significance) and the end of the year, a further radical cleaning of the house takes place. On December 14 in Tokyo, at the Sengaku-ji temple, the suicide of the 47 Ronin is commemorated. Nara once again celebrates a great historic festival in the Kasuga shrine. And so, throughout the course of the year, the Japanese are ceaselessly re-immersed in their history. Finally, after the Christmas trade fair, comes the end of the year: it is time to eat Soba (buckwheat noodles) with a hot soup by the name of Koke, which also means debt. Those unfortunates unable to honor their debts at this point disappear for a few days in order to save face: they will have a new year ahead in which to fulfil their obligations. The last hour of the year is proclaimed by the Buddhist temples with one hundred and eight peals of their great bells. A new life is now to begin, with its procession of rituals and festivals.

Apart from all these public festivities, there are also many particular customs, so great in number as to form an integral part of Japanese civilization. We can do no more here than mention a few of them:
– One should never enter a Japanese house wearing ones shoes: they should be taken off and replaced by a type of slipper. This avoids bringing pollution from outside indoors.
– In reply to a negative question, if one wishes to acquiesce one answers no.
– One offers or accepts an object with both hands. The use of one only shows lack of deference.
– One never passes money directly from hand to hand, except in a shop: it should be presented in an envelope.
– The dozen is a Western concept. In Japan things go in fives and tens (except for bottles of beer and crayons!)
– In a Japanese style inn (Ryokan) it is customary to give tips before and not after one's stay.
– The bath (O-furo) is not a place to wash in but to relax in. One should wash outside the tub and only enter it when one is clean. The water is generally very hot. The whole family bathes in the same water. If you are a guest, you will go in first; this is a mark of honor.
– Nudity is not embarrassing in Japan: if one comes across it one doesn't look.
– One should never stick chopsticks in the rice bowl, because this is how food is offered to the dead.

The habitual way of doing things in Japan often turns out to be the opposite of Western pratices: vegetables are peeled by pushing the knife away from oneself; horses stand with their hindquarters to the back of their stalls; one counts on one's hand by folding one's fingers, not by opening them out; white is the color of mourning, red that of joy; one does not drink with a meal, but before it (Sake) or after it (tea); it is very impolite to open a present in front of the person who has given it to you, and so on. The list could go on forever... but all these little customs are part of the charm of life in Japan. There are not, for all this, any rules, and the Japanese readily forgive any failures of etiquette on the part of a foreigner, always providing that he never loses his smile, under any circumstance.

62. JIDAI MATSURI in Kyoto. On October 22, 794, the emperor Kammu transferred the capital from Nara to Heian-kyo (today's Kyoto). On the 1100th anniversary of this event, the great Heian Shrine (Heian jingu) was established and it was decreed that a great non-religious festival was to be held annually in Kyoto. A procession of over 3,000 people in colorful costumes moves through the streets of Kyoto and represents ten centuries of Japanese history. Jidai Matsuri means the Festival of a Bygone Age.

63. JIDAI MATSURI. Yabusame archer. Yabusame archery became popular in the thirteenth century. The archers were to hit three targets from a galloping horse; those who missed were supposed to commit suicide.

64. GION MATSURI. The Gion is one of the three largest festivals in Japan (together with the Kanda Matsuri in Tokyo and the Tenjin Matsuri in Osaka). It began in 869, when the country was struck by a devastating plague and the emperor ordered the priests and monks of the Yasaka Jinja (Yasaka Shrine) to pray for deliverance. The chief priest organized a procession of sacred objects that were carried through the streets of Kyoto by the young people of the town.

65. MIDOSUJI PARADE, Osaka. This annual parade through the city's streets is more contemporary in character although traditional costumes are not ignored.

66. *JIDAI MATSURI. Men dressed as Samurai, probably from the Edo period. The large straw hats serve also as protection from the elements.*

67. *JIDAI MATSURI. Shinto priests of Heian Jingu.*

68

68. MIDOSUJI PARADE. *Winners of the beauty contest. The blend of traditional and modern is seen vividly in these outward signs of change, not all esthetically pleasing. This American importation is one of the more attractive aspects of change.*

69. *MIDOSUJI PARADE. Yokubue-fuki, a traditional Japanese flute. The oldest form of Japanese music extant is the gagaku in which the flute plays an important part. Later came the fashion for ha-uta and ko-uta, short or long poems read to flute accompaniment.*

70. *MIDOSUJI PARADE. Girl in head gear and hair style from the Heian period.*

71

71. JIDAI MATSURI. Girl in traditional marriage dress.

72. JIDAI MATSURI. Warrior from the Muromachi period (fourteenth century). Note the splendid helmet, designed to strike terror in the heart of the enemy.

73

74

73. *Girls in kimonos celebrating the Seijin-shiki, or coming of age, national holiday on January 15th, when young people aged twenty officially become adults.*

74. *SHICHI-GO SAN. Festival for children three, five or seven years old, which is held on November 15th. On that day boys of five and girls of three and seven go to shrines to pray for a safe and healthy future. There was an ancient belief in Japan that certain ages were prone to bad luck and required more divine protection than usual.*

76

75. *JIDAI MATSURI. Dressed to represent Lord Oda Nobunaga (1534-1582), a great warrior whose conquests brought Japan out of the chaotic feudalism of the time and provided the basis on which the Japanese empire was founded. Nobunaga had the assistance of Hideyoshi, a peasant who entered Nobunaga's service as a groom. Hideyoshi was said to have been as clever as he was ugly and he rose quickly; on Nobunaga's death he became emperor.*

76. *JIDAI MATSURI. Dressed as Abutsu-Ni, a woman of the Fujiwara family who wrote a famous diary (Izayoi-Nikki) of her travels from Kyoto to Kamakura in 1277. The diary, a delightful and sensitive account of her journey, also contains many* waka *(court poems consisting of thirty-one syllables and five verses).*

77

77-78. JIDAI MATSURI. *Dressed as Tomoe Gozen (Lady Tomoe), wife of a famous general in the twelfth century. It was said that she dressed in armor and fought at the side of her husband. At his death she became a nun.*

80

79. *TENJIN MATSURI, a famous water festival held every July in Osaka. It is one the three great festivals in Japan.*

80. *Celebrating Seijin-shiki. The kimono worn today derives from the kosode of the Ashikaga times. At that time it was actually an undergarment worn by the lower classes of society. It was gradually adopted by the upper classes and great attention was paid to the ornamentation of the fabric. There are several types of sleeve for the kimono: the kosode (small sleeve), the osode (large sleeve), the hirosode (wide sleeve) and, most distinctive of all the furisode (hanging sleeve), all in use today.*

143

81. JIDAI MATSURI. A Yabusame archer.
The choice of the bamboo for the arrow is extremely important: it must be strong but supple and the balance must be perfect. The size of the arrow is considered lucky or unlucky: an arrow of 79 centimeters is thought most propitious. White feathers on the arrow are believed to chase away evil spirits and ensure perfect aim. There is almost a supernatural relationship between a marksman and his bow and arrow. A true master archer observes strict rules of meditation and prayer before performing; the traditional cry of kiai, *the expression of spiritual energy, is always used as the arrow leaves the bow.*

82

144

82. *JIDAI MATSURI. Waiting for the parade to begin.*

83. *JIDAI MATSURI. A fourteenth century warrior. As far back as the tenth century a hereditary class of Bushi or warriors existed. The importance of these Bushi or Samurai (meaning "one who serves") grew until the whole country was under their power. The privilege of bearing arms was largely restricted to the Samurai whose power lasted well into the nineteenth century.*

84. *MIDOSUJI PARADE. Taiko folk drummer.*

85. *JIDAI MATSURI. Dressed as Shizuka-Gozen (quiet lady), a famous dancer who was the mistress of Yoshitsune, brother of the emperor Yoritomo. It was largely through the military genius of Yoshitsune that Yoritomo gained the throne, but once in power he ordered the death of his brother, whom he considered a dangerous rival.*

86. *MIDOSUJI PARADE. Spectators.*

87

87. *MIDOSUJI PARADE. Tiger Girls. Baseball is one of the favorite sports in Japan and one of the most popular teams is the Hanshin Tigers. These girls march in support of their favorite team.*

88. *MIDOSUJI PARADE. Girl dressed as a butterfly for good luck.*

89. *MIDOSUJI PARADE. Brass band.*

88

89

The Rural Scene

Life in the country

The Japanese countryside retreats further and further as buildings relentlessly encroach upon rural land. It has to be said, however, that the agricultural population represents no more than ten percent of the labor force. Arable land is scarce. Rice is the staple foodstuff, and flat ground is needed for its cultivation; so village houses generally hug the foothills, releasing as much land as possible for crops. Fields are tiny, and crossed by little earth paths. Hill tops are always well-wooded, and often shelter a small temple or shrine, whose great tiled roof rises among the foliage. Most village houses have a first floor (or second, if, like the Japanese, you call the ground the first storey) and nowadays they are roofed with tiles in red, blue, green, yellow, adding a touch of color to the undulating wave of rooftops. Sometimes fields lie interspersed among houses, even on the outskirts of large towns, and are tended as carefully as gardens. At harvest time, rows of corn sheaves are lined up on posts to dry in the sun. One never sees haystacks piled high as in Europe. But there are all manner of vegetables, including white cabbages and *daikon* (a type of white radish). Everything is scrupulously washed before being offered for sale. Most agriculture is now mechanized and farmers use tiny tractors and motorized ploughs. The same fields are alternately flooded for rice cultivation and used to grow market garden produce, wheat, or other crops. Like its inhabitants, the earth never rests, except perhaps in the north of the islands where the climate is too cold to permit the rotation of crops. In these northern regions, fruit trees are cultivated instead, yielding apples, pears, cherries.

In mountain areas one still finds village houses with traditional roofs, but little by little these are disappearing, giving way to solidly built houses roofed with tiles, as everywhere else. The villagers in these remote parts, far removed from the great urban centers, still keep alive their old traditions and costumes, often continuing to wear regional dress, even at work in the fields. Depending on area and altitude, they produce fruit, tea, tobacco, and even continue to rear silkworms. Some villages concentrate their labors on woodcutting, while others turn to tourism in the winter months, functioning as ski resorts. In the island of Kyushu plums are cultivated on the mountain slopes, while the low ground yields two crops of rice per year. Some villages in central Honshu have vast greenhouses in which flowers are cultivated, chiefly chrysanthemums, of which there are a thousand varieties, highly prized by the Japanese. Life in the villages is no less busy than in the towns, although the pace may seem slower, being determined more by the seasons and the sun than by the clock. The raising of cattle, and even

90. TANABATA FESTIVAL. Celebrated on July 7th, this festival harks back to an old Chinese story of two stars which represent a shepherd and a girl in love. It is the custom to place paper ornaments or lanterns on bamboo sticks in their honor.

more so of poultry, is highly developed in Japan and constitutes the main occupation of entire villages, particularly in the north. But whatever type of farming or other work the country people engage in, they have a very high standard of living, comparable to that of town dwellers, and their roof-tops bristle with television aerials. While they may have to go to the nearest town to find a department store, each village nonetheless has shops and cafés, often even a cinema.

Coastal villages differ little from those inland, except of course in their primary occupation, which is fishing. Most boats are motorized and, outside the large ports engaged in deep-sea fishing, the fishing villages are busy throughout the year. The Japanese diet is based on rice and fish, and the waters of the Pacific are well-stocked, so fishermen have no cause to be idle. And every little bay and cove shelters a little village. For all that, whether fishermen or farmers, the Japanese are not content to confine themselves to their main occupation. While the husband is in the fields or out at sea, the wife often carries on a little business or craft of her own. The villages thus function at the same time as producers and centers of trade. Decentralization being the rule in Japan, the factories that process farm or ocean produce are often situated close to their source of raw material, providing work for most of the local population in times when none needs doing in the fields or the weather is unfavorable. This additional economic activity gives Japanese villages a character very different to that we know in the West. As a general rule women work together with men, often carrying out the roughest jobs. The culture of pearls is but one of the supplementary activities carried on in fishing villages, a mere handful of which specialize in the breeding of pearl oysters. Although they are relatively few in number, the pearl fisherwomen of Japan are famous throughout the world. As for deep-sea fishing, this is performed on an industrial scale, as in other countries, with modern ships and methods. Snow, which covers much of northern Japan in a thick blanket throughout the winter, brings farming to a halt and restricts fishing: but it does not for all this reduce the Japanese to idleness. Roads, railways and roof-tops constantly have to be cleared'. Many mountain villages function as ski resorts, and the villagers transform themselves into hoteliers and ski instructors, and pursue all manner of seasonal activities. Those who have no vocation for tourism, turn to crafts. Each farm has a little workshop producing, for example, *kokeshi*, little dolls without arms or legs, decorated by hand, or *geta*, wooden clogs, or pieces for games, fans, lanterns, quality paper and cloth, indeed a wide variety of goods. Some villages are reputed for their pottery and ceramics, others for their dyeing of material. Still others specialize in the craft of lacquered or wood furniture, or the firework industry. Whether they live in the town or country, the Japanese have a horror of inactivity and, if they are great consumers, they also have an overwhelming drive to be producers: it is a matter of pride.

Certain villages still keep the old traditions and ways of life very much alive, with special dances, music and styles of dress. None of which stops them from pursuing, side by side with the old customs, a way of life that is altogether modern. Because, basically, what is most striking about Japan, is the constant juxtaposition of the most traditional of pasts and the most modern of presents. Nothing replaces anything else, everything is superimposed, in the most harmonious way possible. Except, as happens elsewhere in the world, when hideous corrugated iron takes the place of romantic thatched roofs.

Inlaid wooden box, from the Nara period (eighth century). Imperial Household Agency.

Arts and Crafts

The Japanese have always excelled in all arts and crafts requiring dexterity and know-how, and the quality of their work has rarely been matched elsewhere, whether one considers their metal-work, ceramics, lacquer work or the many little objects which constitute part of the charm of everyday life.

Objects in wood, a material in which the Japanese have worked since prehistoric times, are extremely various, ranging from numerous types of box – of extremely well-finished construction – to articles of bamboo, a supple material which lends itself equally to the making of pots and remarkably delicate jewelry. Wood engravers, with scrupulous exactitude and much talent, knew how to reproduce the tiniest details of a picture or calligraphy: old wood blocks are now much sought after by collectors. But wood was also used in making dolls and objects of popular worship, as well as masks for Noh theater and musical instruments: its applications in Japan are infinite.

Metal-work is equally varied. While bronze was often reserved for objects of worship, iron, at least from the fourth century on, was used to make armor and weapons. One can still marvel at the sumptuous Japanese armor of the time of the Samurai, composed of plates of lacquered iron laced together with cords of colored silk, and admire the decoration of the helmets, the masks of war, the arrowheads of perforated iron. But it was the swords that were forged with the greatest love, with religious care and attention, by specialist craftsmen. The sword, the very soul of the Japanese warrior, was a treasure from which death alone could separate him. It was handed down from father to son like a precious inheritance. The craftmanship of the iron blade was of the very best. As early as the eighth century Japanese iron-smiths showed a great skill. But it was above all in the Heian and Kamakura periods that the forging of blades reached a degree of perfection never to be exceeded. These *koto* (old blades) are unique works of art. During the Ashikaga period they began to be sumptuously fitted with decorated hilt-guards (*tsuba*) and other trimmings, each more splendid than the last, which transformed swords into objects of great value. The Edo period brought no improvement in forging techniques, only in the decoration of the *tsuba*, hilts and scabbards. After 1530 the swords were called *Shinto*, that is to say "new blades." From 1877 they were made only for military parades and these newly wrought objects, the pride of soldiers in modern war, bore only the name *Shin-shin-to* (entirely new blades).

The first Japanese swords (*tsurugi*) had a straight blade. This came gradually to be replaced by a short blade with a single cutting edge.

When the sword was not in use, its blade was ritually dismantled, cleaned and put away in a special scabbard of magnolia wood. It was then fitted with a hilt of the same wood, but the hilt-guard (*tsuba*) was removed and put reverently to the side. Extreme care was taken of the sword, to protect it from getting scratched or rusted. The great ceremonial sword (*tachi*), worn attached to the belt, had a very fine and curving blade. During the Ashikaga period it was replaced by the *katana*, a more solid, only slightly curved weapon, which was slipped inside the belt, cutting edge upwards. The Samurai generally accompanied it with another sword, the companion (*wakizashi*), similarly tucked into the belt. There were also other, very short swords (*tanto* and *aikuchi*, among others), which were more daggers than swords and restricted to female use. The *aikuchi* had no hilt-guard. The worth of a blade corresponded to the quality of its steel, forged numerous times in multiple layers, and to the tempering of its edge (*yakiba*) whose design was particular to each smith. The study of Japanese sword blades is still a long and difficult undertaking and real connoisseurs are rare outside Japan. As for the *tsuba*, the delight of collectors, they are thick plates of magnificently wrought iron, often encrusted with gold and silver, the works of the most reputed craftsmen. They are infinitely various in form and decoration, no two being alike. Excellent reproductions of them are now made.

The craft of metal-work was not confined exclusively to weapons. From the time of Christ bronze alloys were used in making mirrors based on Chinese models, decorated on the back with various motifs, and also in forging bells for the monasteries. Different alloys were used in making utensils and metal objects required by the temples and the aristocracy. Buddhist statues were embellished with delicate gold and silver work and temple pillars and furniture soon came to be decorated in a similar manner. Door handles, the tops of posts, the ends of beams, were ornamented with engraved and perforated metal-work. The crafts of the foundry and forge allowed the Japanese successfully to imitate the first arquebuses introduced to Japan in 1543 and, in the Edo period, there was a great craze for all sorts of objects in wrought metal, hair-pins, braziers, holders of incense and scent, kettles for the tea ceremony, steel tinder-boxes, pipe bowls, belt buckles, various ornaments and accessories of the Buddhist religion (resonant cups, for instance, requiring a special alloy). Smiths strained their ingenuity contriving little jointed animals in iron, worked with extreme precision, dragons, insects, crabs, birds, etc., to gladden the eyes of the nobility. Alloys were also used in making vases, simple in form, delicately ornamented with animals or flowers of exquisite craftmanship. The first real clock arrived in Japan in 1609. It was quickly imitated, but only monks made use of the clocks, adapting the divisions of the clock-face to their needs.

One of the most flourishing of the arts in Japan, metal-work apart, was ceramics. While pottery had been known in the country since prehistoric times, it was not till the period of the Kofun that the first glazed pots appeared, the "Sue," imported from Korea. Tile work did not come in until the end of the sixth century. Ceramics underwent no great development, however, before the sixteenth century. In the fifteenth century the vogue of the tea ceremony provoked a revival of the craft of pottery, in imitation of Chinese models, but the resulting bowls were only of moderate quality. The real blossoming of Japanese ceramics came at the end of the sixteenth century, when Korean potters established themselves in the country and set up their kilns in a number of places. They started by making tea bowls in large numbers to meet the needs of the nobility. From the very start different styles emerged, originating from the Kyoto area (the kilns of Seto, Tamba and others) and from Kyushu (pottery of the Karatsu type). The most highly prized tea bowls and jars were then the "Rakuyaki," which were slightly rustic in appearance. Each potter had his own style and one needs to be a specialist to distinguish between the work of the kilns of Shino, Oribe, Bizen, Tamba, Tokoname and others, all flourishing at the beginning of the seventeenth century. It was a ceramist by the name of Kakiemon (early seventeenth century) who first produced colored porcelain in Japan, in the kilns of Arita and Imari in Kyushu. This type of porcelain was quickly imitated elsewhere and the fashion for it became widespread. It was exported in great quantity to Europe and came to be copied in Delft and in France, chinoiseries then being much in vogue. Other potters set themselves up in the provinces, producing a variety of objects in decorated porcelain, such as the Kutani, and they either imitated Chinese work or, on the contrary, tried to create pieces of typically Japanese manufacture. Influenced by the Chinese ceramics of the Qing period, the work of the Japanese potters became more refined. Putting to use the talents of local painters, such as Korin or Kenzan, they developed new styles, deliberately abandoning those of the Yi dynasty of Korea, and pleasing the tastes of the nouveaux riches of the Edo period. In Kyushu, the Nabeshima kilns were soon bringing forth pieces regarded as the finest work of the Japanese ceramists, as much for the elegance of their shapes as for the beauty of their decoration. In the eighteenth century the Hizen kilns produced a new type of ceramic, whose decoration was inspired by European painting which had become known through the agency of traders living in Nagasaki. But it was in the Kyoto area that the artists were most productive, ceaselessly perfecting their techniques and varying their themes. At the start of the nineteenth century Japanese ceramics was one of the most flourishing of the arts, the demand for quality pieces constantly increasing. The provincial kilns strove to imitate the productions of those in Kyoto and the Kutani style had a renewed success. Ceramists then sought to rediscover the old formulas and invent new shapes and decorations. But with the arrival of Europeans in the middle of the nineteenth century the art of ceramics suffered a sharp decline. There followed a move away from Japanese works in favor of Western ones, with a consequent loss both in quality and originality. The art of ceramics, which continues to be practised in Japan by a fairly large number of craftsmen, has been modernized and, though lacking in originality, is still of very high quality.

Lacquer, known in Japan since at least the fifth century B.C. and extensively used in the sculpture of the Nara period, was brought to a high degree of perfection by Japanese artisans, who invented numerous processes for the decoration of all sorts of ordinary and luxury objects. Lacquer was used to cover temple pillars, furniture, musical instruments, boxes and a variety of chests, as well as in the making of bowls and everyday receptacles. Wood, cloth and leather could all be lacquered. But the most outstanding of the techniques in use was the decoration that characterized Japanese lacquer work: painting, mother-of-pearl inlay, gold and silver leaf, yielding results of astonishing richness. The still wet lacquer was sprinkled with gold or silver (*maki-e*) or scattered with little pieces of metal (*kirikane*). Pictures, imitating the

Noh theater costume. This type is called Surihaku and is used for female roles. From the Momoyama period (early seventeenth century). National Museum, Tokyo.

artistic styles then in vogue, were painted on the lacquer and high-lighted with precious metals and mother-of-pearl. During the Kamakura period (1192-1333), the basic object was first shaped in wood, then coated with several layers of lacquer of varying degrees of thickness. This *taka-maki-e* lent itself to delicate workmanship: cosmetic boxes, painted trays, saddles, and so on. From the sixteenth century on, the ornamentation developed according to the trends in decorative painting: the basic objects, generally of black lacquer, were decorated in gold or in oil colors. Then leaf of various metals, lead, tin, even copper, was used in the composition of increasingly intricate motifs. Whereas, before the Edo period, lacquer was primarily a speciality of Kyoto craftsmen, it later spread throughout the provinces and soon the Edo craftsmen surpassed those of the capital. After 1868, however, suffering a little from neglect, the craft of lacquer retreated to the provinces where many workshops were set up, each with its individual style of decoration. Nowadays the craft of lacquer has joined that of enamel, being practised only by a few rare craftsmen working primarily for the export market.

The craft of textiles was probably imported from China or Korea in the fourth or fifth centuries. But it was with the introduction of Buddhism in the sixth century that textile arts, specifically embroidery, began to develop. The rich silks imported from the continent stimulated the Japanese to rival them: weavers and dyers competed in talent to provide the court with sumptuous materials in delicate colors, highly prized by the nobles and ladies of the court. Various dyeing techniques were then invented or adapted from those in use in China, as well as methods of weaving. But it was in the Momoyama period (end of the sixteenth century) that clothes began to be embellished with designs embroidered in gold and silver thread, particularly the splendid costumes worn in Noh theater. The workshops of Kyoto produced colored brocades, Nishiki, which were in constantly increasing demand. New styles of dress were imported from abroad, such as coats and jackets. But it was the Edo period that brought the greatest changes of fashion: the townsmen (Chonin) wanted to imitate the Samurai and dressed more and more luxuriously. Techniques of weaving, dyeing and embroidery were perfected and textile mills constructed for the mass production of new silk and cotton fabrics. Wool was not imported until the end of the nineteenth century, with new European weaving looms and industrial dyeing methods. Textile arts will survive in the modern world as long as the kimono still exists. However the craftmanship which has established the reputation of Japanese textiles is waning in the face of modern techniques and fabrics, and the gradual abandonment of traditional dress.

91. HATAKE (field with vegetables). In Japan only about 15 per cent of the land is suitable for cultivation, as opposed to around 40 per cent in most European countries. On the whole climactic factors are favorable to agriculture in Japan, but unfortunately most of the land is not very fertile.

92. DAN-DAN-BATAKE (terraces of tea and vegetables). The Japanese are great tea drinkers and most people drink between ten to twenty cups a day. At one time Japan exported tea, but nowadays tea exporting is no longer an important part of the Japanese economy.

93. Sulphur steam springs near Mount Fuji.

94. Rice paddy. By far the largest and most significant crop in Japan is rice. The paddy fields require a huge amount of water and are supplied by an elaborate irrigation system which keeps the field submerged to a depth of about three inches when the crop is young. The fields are drained right before harvesting time.

95. Harvesting rice. The age-old system of hand cutting with its back breaking labor is slowly being replaced by machines.

96. HOSHIGAKI (dried persimmons).

97. Autumn leaves changing colors. With its plentiful rainfall, Japan is a well wooded country; in fact, over half the total area of the country can be classified as forest.

98. TOGYU. Bullfight in Uwajima (Shikoku). The fight takes place between two bulls and blood is rarely shed. The bulls themselves are greatly admired and are accorded ranks commensurate to their ability to win fights. Heavy betting takes place during the fight.

99. Making waraji (Japanese sandals), of rough straw with a thong that passes between the big and second toe.

100. Making waribashi (chopsticks). The chopsticks are made of a single piece of wood that is broken into two (hashi) before eating.

102

101. *SHIRAITONO-TAKI (White Thread Falls). Spectacular falls at the foot of Mount Fuji on the upper reaches of the Shibakawa River.*

102. *Traveling down a canal.*

179

103

103. *Collecting old paper.*

104. *Harvesting rice. The Japanese farmer manages to get more out of his land than most European or American farmers, and two or even three times the amount of other Asiatic farmers.*

105. *CHABATAKE (tea field) in Kyushu.*

104

105

106

107

106-107. Healing a sick tree in the village of Kurama.

108. Preparing a fish net. Fishing is one of Japan's most important industries. The Japanese are great fish eaters and the main source of protein in the Japanese diet is provided by fish.

108

Sports and Martial Arts

The main leisure activity of the Japanese, young and not so young included, is sport. They are great fans of Sumo, the national wrestling. Its annual tournaments draw enormous crowds and hold the spellbound attention of millions of televiewers. There is equal enthusiasm for team games and individual ones, the top favorites being American baseball and golf. Baseball is popular above all with the young, and school and university teams attract supporters all the more fervent for having once played in this or that baseball team. Special stadiums are given over to this game and on Sundays, wherever an empty space is to be found, boys practise hitting the ball and catching it correctly in gloved hands. One often comes across the young playing like this, sometimes with neither bat nor glove, rehearsing the proper movements. It is the same with golf. As there is little ground available to provide a green with nine or eighteen holes, the Japanese have dreamed up rectangular areas, completely surrounded by green nets, where on one, two or even three floors men and women can practise hitting balls supplied to them by an automatic machine. One even finds practice grounds on the roofs of department stores. Because of the lack of space, roofs are often put to use as sports grounds (for tennis, golf or other games) and are also fitted out as children's playgrounds. All Western sports are played in Japan, with the keenness that the Japanese invest in everything they do. For all that, they do not neglect their national sports, especially now that these have become so popular internationally: Judo, the Mecca of which is Kodokan in Tokyo; Aikido and Karate, which are also practised abroad. The most traditional of sports prove popular with the young of both sexes: Kyudo (an assymetrical form of archery) and Kendo (the art of the sword), which requires armor and a type of helmet to be worn and is practised, to the accompaniment of great cries, with a wooden sword, the Shinai. Apart from sport, Japanese youth love travel; whenever they have a holiday, groups of boys and girls set off with their knapsacks on their backs to visit a mountain or a part of Japan unknown to them. In winter they go, still in groups, to take part in winter sports. During their vacations they prefer to go away on school expeditions. Grouped by classes, and with their teachers as guides, they visit the high regions of Japan. Particularly in autumn, tourist sites are congested with coaches and thousands of boys and girls in uniform following their guides, who summon them by blowing whistles and waving little flags.

What about the Geishas, you might ask? Like Noh, Kabuki, Sumo, the tea ceremony, they are living witnesses to times gone by, traditions now carefully nurtured lest they die out prematurely. There are little over

109. Winter scene in northern Japan.

a hundred geishas in Tokyo, perhaps a few more in Kyoto, the imperial city. Like the temples and the emperor, they remain as precious relics of the past, without which Japan would not be quite the same.

The origins of the martial arts

The very popularity of the Japanese martial arts makes them a difficult subject to approach. Their different forms, Judo, Aikido, Karate, archery (Kyudo), Kendo, are wholly recent. The suffix "do," which means "the way," has replaced "Jutsu," the suffix of the old martial techniques. It was only after the Meiji revolution (1868) that the former Samurai, who no longer had a full-time occupation, came gradually to contemplate organizing public demonstrations of their art and techniques, up to this point guarded as the closest of secrets. The considerable success of these demonstrations with the Japanese public led many masters to adapt the martial techniques to more spiritual forms. In 1882 Master Kano Jigoro opened the first school of Judo and gradually developed his particular method, to which he gave the name Kodokan-Judo. (Kodokan: school of the study of the way, and Judo: way of suppleness). It was an adaptation of Ju-Jutsu, a technique intended to achieve the rapid defeat of an adversary by violent torsion of the limbs and brutal throwing. From this point on Judo laid emphasis on physical and mental mastery. The rules of Judo allow combatants to grab, throw, pin each other to the ground, to twist arms or legs, on condition that no one is injured and the rules of courtesy are respected.

In 1927, Ueshiba Morihei, Master of Ju-Jutsu of the Daito School, founded his first school of Aikido. Such was its fame that many masters of Judo and Kendo figured among his pupils. In 1922, an expert in bare-handed wrestling from Okinawa, Master Funakoshi Gishin, gave a demonstration of Karate. Two years later, the University of Keio established the first Dojo (school of martial arts) of Karate in Japan. This form of combat is a synthesis of all the martial arts related to Karate: Okinawa-te, Kenpo, T'ai-Chi, etc. It succeeded Karate-Jutsu, which, pronounced according to Chinese ideograms, meant "art of the hands." "Kara," meaning "China," was replaced by an ideogram pronounced in the same way but meaning "empty." Thus originated contemporary Karate or "The Art of Empty Hands."

These three examples illustrate the transition from techniques of combat (Bugei) to Budo (from Bu: warrior and Do: the way, thus the way of the warrior). But Bu also meant reconciliation and harmony. Thus the martial arts, or Budo, had a further meaning, "the way of harmony."

The old Samurai schools, most often buried in the depths of the countryside, rapidly lost their importance, but a certain number of them have survived even to this day.

In 1843, the Shogun for the first time ordered a count of the great schools of Japan. They were reckoned at 159 (of which, 61 for the sword, 29 for bare-handed combat, 14 for archery, 9 for riding and 5 various).

In actual fact, there were in existence in Japan a good many clandestine schools, remote little schools and roving warriors who occasionally gave lessons: they were known as Bushi. These warriors were in some cases seasoned masters, but lacked followers. It sometimes happened that, in passing, they came into confrontation with masters from the famous, well established schools and defeated them. The superiority of these warriors, which Miyamoto perfectly indicates, came from their

Yoroi type armor, from the Kamakura period (late twelfth century). Mitake Shrine, Tokyo.

continual training, from constant practical confrontation with harsh reality, whereas the masters of the Ryu schools of martial arts, were liable at times to fall asleep while expounding their theories.

It remains nonetheless true that the secret teaching of the Ryu has come down to us only in tiny driblets. These schools still stand as the symbols of an esoteric martial tradition, closed in on itself, surviving to this very day, or disappearing when certain of its members die and books and texts bequeathed to them by a whole line of masters are destroyed.

They hold, rightly or wrongly, that there is no one today worthy to carry on the tradition.

These old schools of the martial arts have never been made the subject of proper study. The secrecy with which they surround themselves, continuing to this very day, permits only an external approach. And yet the Ryu, essentially scattered throughout the countryside, have played an important role in Japanese history. It was often around a Ryu and its masters that the life of a village gravitated. Festivals, tournaments, all sorts of happenings, involved the villages in the life of the Ryu.

The study of these Ryu, their traditions, the texts and teachings of the masters, would be a valuable source of knowledge and bring to the light a fascinating and unknown side of Japan.

The founding of the oldest school in Japan, the Katori Shinto Ryu, brings to mind a fairy tale. It is attributed to Izasa Chosai (1387-1488), a valiant Samurai who practised Shintoism.

One day, when he found himself in the shrine of Kashima and Katori, dedicated to Futsu Nushi, the god of war, it occurred to Chosai to wash his horse's feet in the temple fountain. Instantly the horse fell dead.

Izasa realized that he had just committed sacrilege: the water of the shrine was reserved exclusively for the purification of the faithful. As a gesture of repentance, he shut himself in the temple for a thousand days, devoting his time to meditation and the art of the sword. He thus had the time to perfect new rules of combat, which were to give birth to the school of Tenshin Shoden Katori Shinto Ryu, known as the school of Katori, which he founded when his time of penitence was over.

From this time on, the tradition was perpetuated, handed down from father to son. Today, the heir to the dynasty, by the name of Yasusada, still too young and inexpert, is trained by the Master Otake, who presently directs the school. His adherents number about a thousand, scattered throughout Japan, and his initiates less than thirty.

The handing down of secrets is in effect extremely strict: the initiate has to sign with his own blood (after a light pricking of the finger) an undertaking to reveal nothing of what he has learned. "That also is a secret," says Master Otake, smiling.

The training lasts for a good number of years. During the first three, the pupil has to practice exercises and at the end of the period receives his first diploma. Then, three or four years later, a second diploma follows. Finally, those who manage to attain a certain level, are entitled to initiatory instruction, part of which are the nine signs necessary to concentration.

Meditation is done in the Zazen or seated position. And as for the spiritual teaching, one sentence sums it up: "If one starts to fight, one has to win," says Master Otake. "But to fight is not the object. Martial art is the art of peace and the art of peace is the most difficult: one must win without fighting."

"For us," said a Japanese industrialist, "Budo, Noh theater, Kabuki are nourishment, our soul is basically very ancient. This is why we can be modern or ultra-modern without losing our roots. Nothing in Japan is separate: the light flavor of Sake (rice wine), the taste of raw fish (Sushi), the respect that we pay to our traditions, the veneration we bear to our emperor, all these only make up one Whole. The difference between us and the West is that we have kept a center, or what you call a soul. The center is also the kernel. Without it, the fruit withers and dies."

In effect, Japan still exists as a bridge between old and new. And this is particularly true thanks to the martial arts and the old techniques of combat adopted in new form.

All large companies in Japan are equipped with Dojos (training halls in which thousands of Japanese practice Kendo). The sword is replaced here by three bamboo blades bound together. A helmet and armor protect the head and body. Grace and efficacy, spontaneity and discipline, the rapid and the inflexible, are the common traits of the martial arts. They in fact constitute the very basis of the Japanese soul. It is the art of taking what is to extremes. Because what is lies beyond life and beyond death. It is in being wholly and at all times in what he does that man realizes what he is. Perhaps one should see in these principles the secret of Japanese efficiency, even when it operates in the economic world. It is not generally known that the Meiji emperor, when he did away with the Samurai class and thrust feudal Japan into the age of technology, in fact granted the great merchant families the privilege of economic conquest. Mitsubishi did its utmost to incarnate the Samurai spirit. Its name today is the embodiment not only of the biggest company in Japan, but also of one of the most powerful economic empires of the world.

For the Samurai of old as for today's masters of the martial arts, efficacy is not the ultimate goal. To see is to look into the distance. It is to disregard immediate efficacy for the sake of more lasting future efficacy. We speak in terms of competitiveness, the Japanese in terms of tactics. The Samurai are the incarnation of the secrets of old Japan. But their principles illuminate those of Japan today.

In fact the Samurai spirit has impregnated the Japanese people to such an extent that it underlies all their activities. The rule "pure and hard" has of course suffered erosion by modern Western civilization. But it would be a huge illusion to imagine that Japan has gone to sleep beneath the avalanche of Western technology. Economic competition is also a strategy and the Japanese stand solid and united as a nation when it comes to winning a struggle against anyone whatsoever. During the oil crisis thousands of workers accepted a reduction in salary with applause. The importance of the common cause overcame all else.

For a long time the Samurai enjoyed an unrivalled social role which went as far as to give them rights of life and death over their neighbor. It was the "right to kill and to abandon" (Kirisute gomen) if anyone (peasant or trader) showed them lack of respect. The Samurai had a well-rooted conviction that ordinary people were liable readily to neglect their duties from basic laxity, personal interest, greed for profit, the search for pleasure, hence the obligation to keep them under constant surveillance. The Samurai himself was recompensed with rice and made it a point of duty never to handle money which he considered impure. This trait in fact subsists among the masters of the old Ryu (or schools of the martial arts) who earn their livings by having a second job and never receive money for their teaching.

An understanding of the richness of the Shinto religion is, then, essential to an understanding of the Samurai. By definition they are the warriors of the gods. Underlying and behind all appearances, all combat is sacred combat. Thus, whatever the variations may be, the high and low points of Japanese history, neither the Mongol army, twice strangely destroyed by a sudden typhoon bursting in a clear sky (called divine wind: Kamikaze), nor the West have ever been able to invade Japan. The land of the gods, against the whole world and despite two atomic bombs, has remained inviolate.

Thus the Samurai of yesterday give us the key to the Japan of today. On condition that one sees beyond the brilliant feats of arms and epic poems what without any doubt makes up the astonishing and extraordinary soul of an entire people.

The secret of Ki or energy

One word alone perhaps sums up the basic secret of all the martial arts: the word Ki, which means energy. This word expresses an idea apparently unfamiliar to our Western spirits: that the whole universe is the expression of one and the same force or energy. This energy is identical to ourselves; each being is the result or the vibration of this energy. But we have a being sectioned into parts, namely the physical, psychic and spiritual. If our being was one, if these three parts converged into the same harmony, then our being would no longer be divided, it would wield the cosmic force itself, it would actually be this force or this Ki, and nothing could resist it.

Morihei Ueshiba is undoubtedly one of those who have most perfectly achieved this union of energies or Ki. Although he demonstrated it constantly and, as the creator of Aikido, gave a brilliant display each day, many refused to believe that, up against the wall, subtle force could prove itself superior to brute force.

This is what a powerful adept of Karate said to the master one day.

"Whatever you may claim," he said to him, "you will never manage to convince me. If with my 80 kilos, I strike you with my fist, you will be thrown six meters."

"That will be nothing," said Morihei Ueshiba, who weighed all of 57 kilos.

The Karate-ka insisted to such an extent that they engaged to meet for a public trial. Come the day, and after the customary ceremonials, the Master Ueshiba presented himself with naked torso to his adversary. The latter sprung forward and struck him a great blow in the chest. It was as if he had struck at empty space. Without even flinching, the master smiled.

"Let's start again, I beg you," said the young man, put out of countenance.

He sprung forward a second time and struck with all his might. The master moved no more on this occasion than he had done on the first, but the Karate-ka on the other hand cried out in pain. His wrist had clearly just broken. The lesson was learnt. At the first blow the master had in fact done no more than receive the blow, offering no resistance. The second time he had on the contrary sent back his adversary's own energy, and the latter had in a sense received a return of his own strength tenfold.

Stories of this kind were very numerous in the life of Master Ueshiba. Never could anyone manage to outdo him or catch him out. Whatever

Warrior from the period of the Muromachi Shogunate.

the skill and rapidity of the adversary, he was invariably thrown off, even when the master appeared sleepy, and whatever the angle of attack. One day during the Mongolian war, the master saw a Chinese enemy aim his pistol at him. The man was some six meters away from him. Brusquely and without anyone understanding how, the man was disarmed.

"How did you do it?" he was asked.

"There is a very long time between the moment when the man intends to kill you and the moment when he actually pulls the trigger," was Morihei Ueshiba's reply.

This "very long" time, doubtless a fraction of a second, was sufficient for him to conquer his enemy.

This is to say that the development of Ki gives a different sense of time. In general, one who practices the martial arts feels this phenomenon fairly quickly. For him time no longer has the same span. A little as if the movements of his adversaries reach him in slow motion.

The extraordinary exploits of Master Ueshiba would fill volumes. Not only were many of our contemporaries witness to them, but they were sometimes filmed or photographed. One day when he was unwell, one of his followers wanted to lift him to put him to bed. Unable to manage, he called for help from a second, then a third, then a fourth strong man. They strove in vain to lift the master. He seemed to be nailed to the ground.

Finally he seemed to wake as if from sleep.

"Excuse me," he said. "I had knotted the Sky and the Earth within me." He seemed to relax, and at once they lifted him as lightly as a feather.

These stories are still familiar to the masters of the martial arts.

"I can see if a man has Ki or not, only by his way of walking," says a master.

The most ancient of the martial arts is undoubtedly Sumo. It is the basis of Judo and the old Ju-jutsu. In former times as today combat took place between giants. Many of the Sumotori weighed over 120 kilos and were often over two meters in height. The combats were merciless, lasting to the very death. It was only in 724 that an edict established more humane rules. The training of the Samurai, and hand to hand fighting, were both inspired by Sumo.

The attack is sudden. Its aim is to throw one's adversary outside a circle traced on the ground. But the sudden instant of confrontation between two colossal masses is prepared for at great length. At the great championships the start is often postponed more than ten times. This is an art that only tolerates wholly exceptional practitioners. There are at the most fifty great Sumotori in Japan. The championships give rise to unimaginable suspense, equivalent in the West to that inspired by the European or World Cup in football.

A discipline as much physical as spiritual, the martial arts serve in combat, but above all in the formation of a complete man who has perfect self-mastery. Many masters of the martial arts also have knowledge of acupuncture and the points on the body one can use to cure or to kill. The martial arts are often linked to the study of Zen Buddhism. But in all cases, the spirit of Shintoism, that is to say the veneration of the forces of nature, determines the ritual and symbolic behavior governing all the martial arts. The spirit, the body, reality as a whole, remain in their apparently contradictory aspects an expression of cosmic harmony. This is why the martial arts are as much an art of combat as a school of wisdom.

110. NAGINATA (long sword or glaive) contest. An ancient Japanese weapon, the Naginata is a scimitar-like blade fixed on a wooden haft. Originally only the warrior monks used this weapon, but from the twelfth century on it became a much valued weapon for the foot soldier. Today Naginata competitions are extraordinarily popular and Naginata exhibitions draw large and enthusiastic crowds.

111. In the middle of a Naginata competition.

112

112. KENDO. *A traditional Japanese sport based on the sabre fencing of the Samurai. A fighter is protected by a mask (men), a chest protector (do), quilted panels as thigh protection (tare) and padded gloves protecting the hands and wrists.*

113. *Waiting for the fight at a training school.*

113

114. Attack and defense.

115. Training for martial arts sports begins early in Japan.

116. Professional Samurai in public display of skill. From the tenth century on some warriors devoted their entire lives to the attainment of new skills in sword-play. Formerly, when a man had mastered one style of sword-play, he set out on a tour of the provinces challenging every expert to fight. In the event of defeat he became the victor's pupil.

117. KYUDO (the way of the bow). While Yabusame was primarily mounted archery, Kyudo archery is perfomed in the standing position with emphasis on etiquette and form.

118

119

118. Archery competition in medieval costume.

119. Originally the bow was made of unvarnished boxwood, but later only bamboo was used. For precision of flight, feathers are placed on the arrow; the feathers from eagle's wings are preferred.

120. Sumo wrestling was once confined to local shrines and temples. It became a professional sport in the mid-eighteenth century and acquired the passionate following it still commands today. Here a wrestler is scattering salt at the beginning of a match, as it is believed that salt is purifying.

121. The match takes place on a raised ring with the referee wearing traditional Japanese dress.

122

122. *Student Sumo team waiting for a tournament.*

123. *During the fight a belt is the only clothing permitted. A wrestler of the highest rank is known as a Yokozuna (which is also the name of the belt) and has as large a group of adoring followers as a film star.*

124

125

124. *Full contact Karate; children's competition.*

125. *Judo tournament. This sport, once called Ju-jutsu (Ju meaning pliant and Jutsu meaning technique) is a form of unarmed combat that might be defined as "to conquer by yielding."*

126. *Baseball is one of Japan's most popular sports.*

127

127. Getoboru (gateball, a form of croquet), sport of the elderly.

128-129. American baseball has become enormously popular not only as a spectator sport, but also among the young as a sport of the schoolyard. The "Little League" phenomenon is widely spread.

128

129

130

130. AIKIDO. *The martial art that uses the opponent's strength and weight for one's own defense. Aikido grew out of the old technique of Aiki-jutsu. Leverage, foot action and body work are of the greatest importance, as is a good knowledge of anatomy.*

Entertainment and the Performing Arts

Japanese life, for all that's been said, does not consist entirely of work. The Japanese have a natural gaiety and seize on any opportunity to enjoy themselves and temporarily forget the difficulties of daily life. Apart from the many feasts, festivals and ceremonies that mark the passage of the year, but for the most part are not holidays from work, the Japanese relax in the evenings after work, chatting with their colleagues in bars, which stay open very late; there, over a cup of tea or a drink of Sake (more often a glass of whisky), they can, under cover of mild drunkenness (which excuses everything), temporarily escape the yoke of their duties and obligations, letting themselves go in laughter and song. It is the current vogue to get together for the singing of comic songs, to the accompaniment of a radio or cassette: numerous amateur competitions are held, delighting participants and audience equally. Television has an important place in Japanese life. From early in the morning one national and seven private channels compete for the attention of the employee preparing to go to work and the housewife busy in the house. Children are often spellbound in front of their own channel, which broadcasts endless series of cartoons and stories. At home in the evening the husband watches cultural programs and comedies as well as the news. It is not uncommon in a Japanese house to find a television in every room, which allows everyone, to the obvious detriment of family life, to watch the program of their choice. The average Japanese, having spent all his day in group activity, is thus able to isolate himself and, through the medium of the screen, dream a little and escape into a different life.

On their days off the favorite pastime of the Japanese is to stroll in the streets, window shop, and in good weather admire flowers and visit temples. Not from extreme religiosity, but as much out of respect for the divinities – whichever they might be – as for the tranquil beauty of temple architecture and gardens. People also frequent exhibitions, of art, flowers, antiques, indeed anything at all, held in specialist galleries, museums, temples and department stores. The latter generally devote a floor to temporary exhibitions, often of high quality, drawing crowds of visitors of all ages. There is no proper ministry of culture in Japan and the State almost never intervenes in the cultural field. Virtually all patronage is private and artistic events in all fields are sponsored by industrial or commercial companies, chain stores or newspapers. As a result, all artistic and literary movements are free to develop at will: it is for the public to choose, not for the government to impose. Culture in Japan is not the province of a powerful elite but of the general public. Thus the whole population participates in the country's cultural development at every level. The extensive entertainment districts found in all large cities, Shinjuku in Tokyo, for example, with bars packed together, Pachinko arcades (a type of mechanical ball game), sex-shops, cabarets, cafés and other places of amusement, so well frequented that on Sundays cars are forbidden access, are as much a part of the general cultural life as (on a different level) the cinema or theater. While cinemas exist in abundance, theaters are less in evidence. They stage European and American works or traditional ones such as Kabuki, in which song, music and dance all play an integral part. The Noh plays are relatively exceptional, being part of the cultural tradition it is important to preserve, although most Japanese find them profoundly boring. They go to watch Noh all the same, as it is the done thing to honor with one's presence an artistic production that keeps tradition alive. People more readily enjoy Kabuki, which has greater appeal to popular taste, or Bunraku, a puppet show staged relatively rarely but highly esteemed. Music is very popular in Japan and concerts of Western music are very well attended: Japan has a number of high class symphony orchestras. In some cafés music is played, discreetly so as not to disturb the clientele, ranging from classical to jazz to traditional Japanese tunes. The young are strongly drawn to contemporary American music and in certain establishments they can dance in the evening to the deafening sounds of Reggae, Free Jazz or Rock. Cabarets and nightclubs are well attended, especially by men who are drawn there both by the lavishness of the shows and the motivated courtesy of the "hostesses." Japanese men, often suffering from love troubles, will sometimes spend an evening in a "bar" where they are given a gracious welcome by a series of hostesses who are there only to give each individual the impression, for a few hours, that he is a celebrity, surrounded by amiability, given every attention.

The cinema appeals mainly to the young. Japanese studios produce many films, most of which are fairly mediocre and of little interest outside Japan, as their subject matter, when it is not purely light entertainment, is mainly concerned with the particular circumstances of Japanese life. Only the best films (often not appreciated in Japan itself) are exported, which explains the high reputation abroad of certain prestigious Japanese producers. The studios, however, work increasingly for television which now absorbs almost all of their production.

A great many Japanese amuse themselves in the evenings taking part in Go or Shogi competitions (Japanese chess) or playing parlor games. There are schools which make a fortune teaching people the art of playing Go, mah-jong or chess.

Music

It is probable that music in Japan has very ancient origins, but we have no knowledge of what they might have been. The first pieces of music, techniques and instruments came, once again, from Korea and China. In Japan it seems that music was at first inseparable from dance and mime, as evidenced by the earliest musical dramas and dances, which were the Gagaku (music of the court) and the ritual dances Kagura and Bugaku of the Nara period. The earliest instruments were the Koto, a type of zither brought from Korea, then the Biwa, a Chinese lute imported in 935. Other flutes, of course, were already in use. Japanese music was not at first written down; each instrument had its individual music, its rhythms and its techniques. Later the Shakuhachi, a flute without a mouthpiece, was brought from China in 1335, followed by the Shamisen from the Ryuku Islands in 1560. These instruments were gradually perfected and eventually led to the production of typically Japanese music. The oldest form of music extant is the Gagaku, which was played with mouth organs (Chinese), flutes, drums and Koto, using a slow rhythm following as closely as possible the sounds of nature. The Noh theater plays are still accompanied by a small orchestra whose job it is to underline the important moments in the drama, which are sung or mimed. Later came the epic songs, performed by a kind of minstrel with Biwa accompaniment. These wandering singers, who were usually blind, had a role in Japan similar to that of our troubadours of the Middle Ages. In the eighteenth century the Naga-uta, or long poems, which came in with the Kabuki theater, were accompanied by Shamisen music. This was followed by the fashion of Ha-uta and Ko-uta, short or long poems sung with flute accompaniment. However, in all cases it was the song or poem whether rhythmical or slow that was of primary importance, and the music itself was strictly accompaniment. While court music remained formal and varied little, a special style of popular music and songs evolved, usually based on themes of work or nature, that used a melodic line. These songs were nearly always accompanied by dances where drums were of fundamental importance. Some Japanese orchestras are, in fact, made up only of drums of various types and very different tonalities: the accent is laid on the rhythm, which is often frenzied. Modern songs, using Western rhythms, are considerably influenced by popular songs and their accents. But one cannot claim that a Japanese music properly existed: the music of ancient times was integrated into the Korean and Chinese, and modern music draws its techniques and themes from the West.

The origins of the theater

In every civilization, theater is religious in origin, and Japan is no exception. One must turn to Shinto mythology, first codified in the oldest historical chronicle of Japan, the *Kojiki* or "Record of Ancient Matters," written in 712, to find this origin. History in story form is entertaining. Vexed and upset by the excesses of her brother Susanoo, the goddess (Kami) of the Sun retreated to a deep cavern and closed its entrance with a large stone, thus plunging the whole world into darkness, to the despair of all the other Kami, who called a council. A goddess, Uzume, came up with a plan: she dressed herself in elaborate fashion and started to sing and dance outside the cavern tapping time on a wooden board with her feet, so as to make as much of a din as possible. While dancing, she assumed erotic poses, which caused the rest of the assembled Kami to burst into fits of laughter. Intrigued, the goddess of the Sun, Amaterasu Omikami, pushed the rock closing her cavern away a little to see what was going on. And she caught sight of her own reflection in a mirror held by Uzume. Thinking that another Sun goddess had supplanted her, she stepped right out of her cave. The other Kami, seizing their chance, at once pushed the large stone back into the entrance to stop her from regaining her den. And the world rejoiced anew at the light of the sun.
It is this erotic dance that lies at the origin of Japanese theater. In the years that followed, many Shinto shrines mimed this scene in the course of their religious celebrations, as well as others drawn from

mythology, notably the Kagura, "music of the gods." These Kagura, enacted in the past by the "descendants" of Uzume who bore the title of Sarumi-no-Kimi at court, are now performed by Miko, sorts of priestesses of the shrines.

From the seventh century on, these ancient religious dances, which were often combined with peasant dances, met with rivalry in the imperial court in the form of different mimed dances imported with Buddhism from Korea. The new dance-dramas, of which there were about ten different types, also essentially religious, were performed on a square stage by masked actors; the spectacle was accompanied by an orchestra comprising a flautist, a drummer and a cymbal player. One of the most famous of the Gigaku dances, which is still performed at many Matsuri (religious feasts), is the "dance of the lion" (Shishi-mai). The other Gigaku dances, however, soon gave place to a different style of dance-drama imported from China, the Bugaku, in which two groups of dancers, one to the left and one to the right, danced different steps to the rhythm of a music known as Gagaku. Each performance was preceded by pieces of Kangen music, in which the mouth organ played an important part. Until at least the thirteenth century, noble courtesans liked to compose Gagaku and Kangen music. In this form of theater, consisting of song and dance, with music as the determining element, one already finds the basic characteristics of the Japanese theatrical tradition, in constant force to this very day: religious content, dance, song and music.

Meanwhile, in parallel with this high class theater, there existed popular forms of peasant drama called Dengaku and Sarugaku, "music of the fields" and "music of the monkeys." These popular dances soon also found favor with Buddhist monks and the nobility, particularly the Dengaku, which were based essentially on music. As for the Sarugaku, which were sometimes put on in the court during perormances of Dengaku and Kangen to amuse the audience, they were principally a type of humorous mime enlivened with acrobatics, to some extent analogous to European medieval "farces," very often erotic.

It was in combining popular dances with the more learned Kangen music that two Shinto priests, Kan'ami and his son Zeami (1363-1444), to satisfy the refined tastes of the Shogun Ashikaga Yoshimitsu, created a special type of theater which, taking on a religious coloring, was to become the supreme art of the court of the Shoguns: Noh.

The art of Noh

Thanks to the patronage of the Ashikaga Shoguns, Noh theater quickly established itself as a noble art. It was to remain the most accomplished expression of Japanese theater to this very day, the actual word Noh meaning at the same time talent and power. There still exist some 240 Noh plays, barely half of which are now performed; most of them are attributed to Zeami or his father. These plays, which have scarcely varied since they were created, either in poetic text (Utai) or sung expression (Yokyoku), can be divided into five groups according to their main subject: those featuring Kami (Shin), the ghosts of warriors (Nan), women (Nyo), mad people (Kyo) or demons of all sorts (Ki). In Noh the actors neither speak nor sing: this is the privilege of a chorus which chants the texts. The roles of the actors essentially involve dancing and meaningful poses, to the accompaniment of a small orchestra. Originally a Noh performance comprised five plays, each

*A wood-block print from the series
"Kabuki Actors on Stage" by Utagawa
Toyokuni, 1794. National Museum, Tokyo.*

Noh mask of the Ko-omote type, used for roles of beautiful young ladies. From the Muromachi period (fifteenth century). Private Collection, Tokyo.

belonging to a different genre, but nowadays the show has generally been reduced to one or two. The opening dance has, nonetheless, been preserved. Called Okina, it is a sort of invocation and a wish for long life, performed by a single actor who wears the mask of an old man and waves a fan. This actor is followed by two more, each different in costume and behavior, thus symbolizing the three stages of life. Then begin the Noh plays themselves (also known as Yokyoku).

All Noh plays have a rigid structure, which allows for no exception: they are divided into three parts known as Jo, Ha and Kyu (beginning, plot, conclusion). At the very beginning appears the Waki, or secondary character, who presents himself so that the audience can situate him. Then the chorus sings a song describing a journey. Next comes the Shite (main character), sometimes accompanied by a Tsure, or minor character. These characters appear to converse with each other (through the agency of the chorus), in such a way as to inform the audience of the plot to follow.

The Shite dances and mimes something that has happened, then withdraws from the stage to give place to a comic interlude, the Kyogen, performed by different actors, sometimes in masks.

The last act brings the reappearance of the Shite, who dances to explain the unfolding and end of the plot.

Only the Shite wears a mask, and sometimes also the Waki when he represents a female character. The masks, of carved wood, slightly smaller than the face of the actor wearing them, are fastened behind the head with a cord. The masks are considered living incarnations of the characters they represent, and as such are revered by the actors as equal to the gods.

The texts, in ancient Japanese, are generally incomprehensible to modern audiences, who are obliged to follow the unfolding of the plot in a booklet.

The highly elaborate costumes are made of silk and very rich brocade. They never vary, their only function being to indicate the status, age and role of the character. Men and women wear a Hakama (a type of wide trouser) called Oguchi, which flares downwards.

Props are simple and few. Apart from the indispensable fan, which can symbolize anything at all according to the actor's part, there are weapons, lances and bows, and particular things characteristic of each play: a boat, a little house, an ox-cart, and so on, all being suggested, rather than recreated, by a light bamboo frame covered in material.

There is virtually no decor. The stage is raised and square, measuring some six meters on each side. The audience is placed in front of the stage and to the left of it. The right of the stage floor, closed off by a balustrade, is occupied by the chorus. At the back are the musicians, drummers and flute player. Behind them, on a large backcloth, is a drawing of a pine. To the rear on the left, a raised passageway, the Hashigakari, its balustrade ornamented by three pines, serves as the actors' entrance and exit. This distinctive stage is covered by a roof, like that of a shrine, supported at the corners by posts which also serve as reference points for the masked actors, whose vision is restricted by their masks.

The Kyogen, which are performed either in the course of each play (between the second and third "acts") or between the different plays, giving the actors time for a change of costume, are inseparable parts of Noh drama: they provide an essential release of the tension built up by the main play, for the exaggerated acting and the often grotesque masks of the players are intended to provoke laughter. Relaxed by the interlude, the spectator can return to the central Noh drama with full concentration.

In the course of the centuries, acting styles developed certain variations and five main schools (Ryu) came to be established, named after their founders: Kanze, Kita, Hosho, Komparu and Kongo. A sixth, more modern, that of Umewaka, was founded in the nineteenth century, but does not seem to have won favor with the public, which tends to regard only the Kange school as truly classical.

While Noh developed principally in aristocratic circles, the townsmen, for the most part prosperous traders, felt enthusiasm for different types of show, which were better adapted to their tastes. For centuries past, bards, accompanying themselves on the Biwa (a type of lute), had sung of the exploits of warriors in times of old, and particularly of those who had had a part in the famous struggle between the Taira and the Heike which ended with the establishment of the Kamakura Shogunate at the end of the twelfth century. These bards, whose tradition has never been lost and continues, in different form, in society today, on the radio as in the streets, were the inspiration, in the sixteenth century, of narratives sung by ordinary people (and even women) accompanying themselves on an instrument newly imported from China, the Shamisen, a type of guitar with three strings. Then Joruri developed, sung stories, which from now on accompanied the popular puppet shows, the Ningyo-shibai, which were, from the nineteenth century called Bunraku, after a puppet-player from Osaka. Puppet theater was introduced to Japan in the ninth century, probably by the Koreans, and was then held in poor esteem. But in the sixteenth century rich tradesmen rediscovered it and transformed the texts of the Ningyo-shibai to suit their tastes. Contemporary life supplied the main themes of the works performed, and they were highly successful. Plays that were violent and vulgar (Aragoto) gradually yielded to more refined works, under the particular influence of Gidayu (1651-1714), who transformed the techniques of Joruri. This is the art that is still highly appreciated in Japan, and also abroad. But popular theater went through an equivalent transformation and, to rival Noh, a Shinto priestess, Okuni, created a type of drama-dance that was half Shinto, half Buddhist; this came to be known by the name Kabuki, meaning "song-dance-actor," and met with enormous success.

Kyogen mask of the Kobuaku type, used for roles of powerful and evil characters. From the Muromachi period (mid-sixteenth century).

Kabuki

It was around 1586 that Okuni danced and sang her Kawara-mono (thing of the river bed) at Kyoto, in the dried up bed of the river Kamo. Having won followers to her art, she included Kyogen actors and Shamisen musicians in her troupe. After her death, she had numerous imitators and, in contrast to Noh plays, where men played every part, in the new Kabuki women could hold the stage. But soon, under the regime of the Tokugawa in the seventeenth century, the presence of women on stage was no longer tolerated and all the characters of Kabuki plays were represented by young men (Wakashu). A new style of Kabuki then emerged, often licentious. Banned in its turn, this type of theater underwent further transformation to become the Kabuki of men (Yaro-Kabuki), then simply Kabuki, which, constantly improved, remains to this day one of the best forms of Japanese theater. It was above all in Osaka and Tokyo (then Edo) that this theatrical form developed, combining music, song, dance, mime, beauty of costume, acrobatic feats, dialogues and "lay" plots, to create a highly colorful spectacle. New stage arrangements were devised, including a larger floor, and performances were held in enclosed places, unlike Noh, which was often performed in the open air.

It was the actor-author Chikamatsu Monzaemon (1653-1724) who gave Kabuki its true spirit. This "Shakespeare of Japan" wrote a great number of plays, some of which were for the Osaka puppet theater, of historical type (Jidai-mono) or recounting contemporary events (Sewa-mono) which met with enormous success. The Kabuki actors did not wear masks, but put on extremely elaborate make-up designed to emphasize the character and type of the persons portrayed. Dance was then somewhat neglected in favor of dramatic action and, at the beginning of the eighteenth century, the roles were classified into eight different types: heroes, villains, heroines, comedians, old men, old women, young men and children. The actors were judged more on their performance than the play on its subject, and acting families became famous. Costumes diversified, stage decors and props grew sumptuous. In 1729, a rotating stage was devised, allowing up to four different settings to be presented. Finally a panoply of equipment providing scenic effects came into use.

But, since the Kabuki plays are based on old texts, it is difficult today to understand them; for this reason a new Kabuki school was recently established, to modernize the acting and texts and introduce new elements drawn from modern techniques. A well-known actor, Ennosuke III, is presently attempting to update Kabuki completely, converting it to a modern show. Many Kabuki actors also work in cinema, which influences the way they act on the stage.

There are presently over ten theaters in Japan exclusively reserved for Kabuki plays, two of which are national theaters in Tokyo and Osaka, putting on from ten to twelve performances each year. There are, naturally, different schools, all seeking to restore to Kabuki the impact it had in days gone by. Because Kabuki, like all other traditional forms of Japanese theater, refuses to become a museum piece. On the contrary, it is striving for a greater popularity than ever before.

In the Meiji era (late nineteenth century), Western forms of theater made their appearance in Japan and many companies were then formed, which either sought to give new life to Kabuki by allowing women to act and re-examining the plots, or on the contrary performed European plays, adopting Western criteria. Typically Japanese subjects were also put on stage, handling political and contemporary themes: it was the school of Sinsei-shimpa which led the way to a determinedly modern theater, first of all with free theater (Jiyu Gekijo), which drew its inspiration from traditional Western pieces, transposed, however, to a Japanese setting, followed, after 1945, by other theatrical forms inspired by those that had developed in Europe and the United States in the post-war period. As a result, one finds in Japanese theater today forms that are resolutely traditional, such as Bunraku and Noh, forms tending to become modernized, like Kabuki, and still others, frankly inspired by Western theatrical norms.

Certain schools also put on avant-garde plays which have nothing to envy works of the same kind staged in the theaters of the West.

131. Actress putting on make-up for a performance.

132. BUGAKU. Traditional Japanese dance, with court music, performed out of doors. This dance-drama form was imported from China.

133

133. NIHONBUYO, a traditional Japanese dance.

134. During the Edo period high ranking courtesans were known as Oiran and lived in a licensed quarter of the city called Yoshiwara. One of the great sights of the city was the parade of the Oiran as they displayed their magnificent clothes and the latest fashions. Yoshiwara was separated from the rest of the city by a large moat and visitors had to secure a special pass to visit it.

135. Geisha dance.

136. SAGI-MAI (dance of the Sagi bird).

137

137. *BUNRAKU. Artist and his puppet. Bunraku first became popular in the early seventeenth century. The three elements of the performance are the puppets, the stylized text recited by a single character and the musical accompaniment of the Shamisen. The puppets themselves are manipulated by sticks and internal springs and are fully equipped not only with arms (introduced in the 1690s) but with moveable eyes, mouths and fingers.*

138. *BUNRAKU. Puppet used to play roles involving mature women. Bunraku was especially admired in Osaka and puppet operators were as sought after as actors.*

139. *Kabuki actor preparing for performance. The stylized make-up that actors wear is an integral part of the Kabuki theater, as are the splendid robes, each designed for a specific role. The actors' costumes had in turn an effect on the dress of the upper classes. The differences in the fashions between men and women's clothes can scarcely be detected.*

140. *Making a television Samurai film in Eiga-Mura, near Kyoto.*

141. *Putting on make-up before going on stage.*

142. *MIKO SAN. Shinto shrine girls.*

143. *Koto players. The Koto is derived from Chinese Gakuso and, like it, has thirteen strings which are tuned by thirteen independent bridges. Theoretically it can produce any scale, although in practice only a few are used. It is played on the floor from a kneeling position and its strings are plucked by three ivory picks attached to the fingers of the right hand.*

144. *Modern night club performers.*

140

141

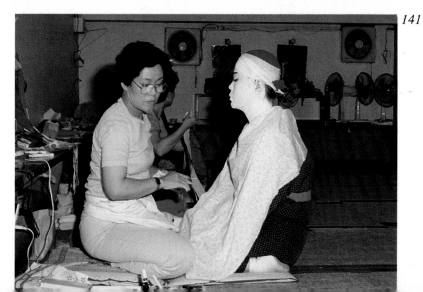

Family Life and Education

Family life in Japan has two very different aspects, depending on whether one considers the town or the country. In the towns the family is utterly separate from the world of work, the latter being regarded as something external, while in the country, work being done in the context of the family, it is not cut off from family life. In towns relatively few married women work, though nearly all unmarried young women who are not at university have a job, whether as office workers, messengers, shop assistants, temporary factory hands, and so on. On marriage a woman generally stops work. She will only take it up again if she is widowed, in order to bring up her children properly. But more and more urban women are taking paid work independently of their husbands. They tend to be intellectuals, artists, or women with a strong creative drive or business flair. Their external activities have to be reconciled to their activities in the home. In the average family, however, it is only the husband who works. He has to earn enough to support his family and bring up his children: this is the limit of his role. He always comes home from work late, either because he is held up in the office or, more likely, because he is dining with his colleagues. When at last he gets home, after a light meal he watches television and goes to bed. Saturdays he also spends with his office colleagues, passing the time in sport or some other amusement. Rarely, very rarely, does his wife join him in his leisure activities. On Sunday, the day of rest, he goes out with his family and can at last enjoy the company of his children, providing of course, that he has not gone away for the weekend with his colleagues. The rare holidays that the Japanese take are spent at the sea-side, visiting family who live far away, or at a thermal station taking the waters. The urban man spends very little time at home. It is his wife who takes care of children, housework, cooking and all practical tasks. Japanese men hate doing jobs about the house: home for them is a place of rest. Fortunately it is easy in Japan to find reliable craftsmen, plumbers, carpenters and other workmen at reasonable cost. In summary, the purpose of marriage is to have children and to bring them up. Conviviality is incidental and, in the towns, there is no proper family life as we know it. The married couple live virtually separate lives and only their children bring them together. It is quite different in the country, where work in the fields or fishing industry involves all members of the family, who form a work unit, it has to be said, rather more than a family unit. Family members are bound to each other by force of tradition, but primarily in the vertical sense: it is only grandparents, parents and children in a direct line of descent who are properly considered part of the family, a spouse

145. A Noh play performed outside on a raised platform. The leading actor is magnificently dressed and wears the traditional wooden mask.

always being regarded as an appendage. A husband and wife are only truly a couple when they have children and all the devotion of the newly established family is concentrated on its offspring, who in this respect are the most coddled in the world. From birth a child is surrounded with every attention and up to the age of four or so is king: nothing is refused him, and he can indulge every whim without attracting the slightest reproof. Then the moment he starts school everything changes. He is obliged to acquire discipline and learn to live in a group. It is the parents duty to instill in him manners, customs and the rules governing social life. Children seldom return home at midday, but take their lunch with them as even nursery school continues until three in the afternoon. At five or six years of age serious study begins: the children leave the nursery school and pass into the *Shogakko*, or primary school, where they spend the next six years. Here they embark on the hard task of learning to write. Thanks to a system of syllabic writing they are able, from the age of four, to read books specially written for them using fifty-one letters. At primary school they memorize and learn to write the Sino-Japanese characters (1850 in all) which, together with the syllabic signs, equip them to read and write. At the same time, from the age of five, they learn to read and write Roman script. There are no exams as such, but a system of continuous assessment. As soon as they get to school in the morning pupils start by doing the housework, with broom, bucket and floorcloth, rendering everything spotless. Classes begin only when all is clean and tidy. Children get to school at 8.30 in the morning and do not leave until 4.30 in the afternoon. They have ten minutes interval every hour, during which they are free to do what they like. The school week lasts from Monday to Saturday with no break in the middle. After school older pupils often attend evening classes, continuing to study until 8 o'clock. At home after dinner they may also have written homework or lessons to learn: the life of a Japanese school child is fully taken up with work, leaving little time for sport or play. School vacations are shorter than in the West. The school year normally begins on April 4 or 5, and continues without a break until July 20, the start of the main annual vacation which ends on August 31. Children must then wait for the winter vacation (December 25 – January 7), followed by that of March 20 – April 4 or 5, which marks the end of the school year.

At the age of twelve or so the child goes to the *Chugakko*, or secondary school. Here he begins to learn foreign languages, specifically English which is' compulsory, and each term is obliged to pass a stiff exam which can last several days. Around the age of fifteen, if he is successful in the entrance exam, the young man goes to the *Kotogakko*, a public or private and fairly expensive school, where he is prepared for university entrance. He spends three years there. When he has obtained his Certificate of Secondary Studies, he can sit the entrance exam of the university of his choice (there are over 1,200 in Japan). If it is a State university, in principle almost free of charge, the exam will be extremely tough, and few pass. Those who fail have the option of applying to a private university, which will be correspondingly higher in cost and lower in its entrance requirements. Since the diplomas of different universities are of varying standard, the jobs that students obtain on completion of their studies depend above all on the quality of the university awarding their final degree. In consequence the entrance exams of the most sought after universities are subject to hot competition and students work unremittingly to succeed. Some families make enormous sacrifices to pay for private courses for their children, and a daughter will often abandon her studies to give her brother a chance of getting into a good university. Overall, children spend their adolescence in much work and little play, apart from participation in major sporting events. They make up for this once they have passed their university entrance exams, and for the next three of four years life is very agreeable. University students have plenty of free time, which is generally spent in group activities centered on membership of sporting or cultural clubs.

At school, uniform is compulsory, but once at university students wear what they please and are no different in this respect from the young of other countries. The kimono is now worn primarily by old women, above all in the country, and Western dress is prevalent everywhere. Nevertheless, at festival times and on ceremonial occasions, men and women return to their national dress, if only for a few hours: the hakama for men, the kimono for women. And on summer evenings and at home everyone wears the yukata, a kimono of light cotton which is much more relaxing than Western dress. If one can in a sense see Western clothes as a symbol of the external aspect of Japanese life, then family life is symbolized by the kimono and yukata.

When a young man, equipped with his diploma, whether from university or secondary school, takes his first job, his behavior changes. Up to this point an individualist, and critical of authority, he now joins the ranks and finds himself obliged to conform to generally accepted rules of behavior, or else risk rejection by his colleagues. On his own, a Japanese is lost: he lacks initiative, having only ever been trained for group activity. And if he is not strong enough to break away from the flock, he will spend his whole life trapped in a spider's web of duties and obligations prescribed by Japanese society: duty to the family and his masters, to his superiors, to the State. At birth a Japanese is accorded no rights, but incurs upon himself an infinite number of obligations which he must fulfil as conscientiously as possible if he is to hold his place in Japanese society. On retirement, generally at sixty years of age, he leaves the active world of production for the passive world of consumption. Apart from the respect due to his years or his knowledge, he now counts for nothing in society, but becomes instead a burden to it. He is given no monthly pension, but on leaving the company to which he has devoted his life's work (in large concerns jobs generally last for life) he receives a large lump sum to dispose of as he wishes. It is up to him to keep active, or spend his days quietly tending his garden, according to his preferences.

Jobs, although they last for life in large commercial and industrial concerns, are often temporary in small companies (which for the most part carry out sub-contracts for large ones). The financial problems of retirement are then harder to solve, although special insurance schemes can help. Social security is a precarious affair, often depending on the good will of company bosses. Every large company has its trade union and local unions are centrally represented, but they have little power vis-à-vis the government. It is the spirit of private enterprise that really governs Japanese society and anyone is free to set up his own business on condition that he succeeds. Bankrupts and the unlucky sometimes combine forces to rebuild a business, because unemployment in Japan is regarded as shameful. And Japanese society shrinks from taking responsibility for those who are without work: it is up to them to make sure that they are not a burden on others.

The Japanese house is welcoming. Whether it is traditional or modern, a sense of intimacy is always preserved, vast openings generally giving onto a tiny garden, scrupulously tended by the master of the house: for all self-respecting Japanese men, though they may scorn jobs about the house, are gardeners. The Japanese prefer to live in Houses rather than in flats, if they can afford them. A good many workers and minor employees have no choice but to live in blocks of cheap accommodation; however, as soon as they are able to, they buy or build a little house outside town. Suburbs may stretch as far as 30-40 miles, but this poses little problem as there is always appropriate transport. These little houses generally have a ground and first floor. To make the most of space, which is always at a premium, at least one room on the ground floor is covered with Tatami, traditional straw mats, while the other rooms are tiled or scattered with carpets in Western style. It is in the Tatami room that the Tokonoma is situated: a special alcove decorated with a Kakemono (a traditional vertical painting) and a vase of flowers, which vary according to the season. This is the most formal room, in which distinguished guests are made welcome in Japanese style. In the other reception rooms, which normally communicate with the kitchen (Dai-dokoro, the principal place), the furniture is now normally of Western style: tables and chairs, armchairs and piano. The bedrooms are on the first floor and almost always furnished with Tatami, on which thin mattresses called Luton are unrolled at night. In the daytime the Luton are housed in large cupboards which can accommodate all furniture necessary. Bedrooms are relatively bare, apart from the children's room which is equipped with a desk and bookshelves. At the entrance to the house there is a small area where the family and visitors take off their shoes when they come in, and exchange them for slippers. The bathroom has for the most part remained traditional in style, although made in modern materials; the tub of the O-furo, whose water is kept constantly hot by gas or electricity, is now generally made of enamel, though occasionally still of wood (which is increasingly a luxury). Beside it is a little alcove in which to undress, also housing the washing machine. The kitchen is not very different from Western kitchens except in the range of its household utensils. In traditional houses, of which there remain a great number on the outskirts of cities and in provincial towns, one still finds Fusuma, mobile partitions which allow the size of rooms to be altered. Woodwork is never painted: it would be viewed as sacrilege – and, moreover, an error of taste – to mask wood's warm and polished surface, which bestows an air of intimacy and calm on the Japanese house, where nothing should assault one's gaze. When the Fusuma on the outside wall are opened, the inside of the house gives directly onto the garden, which is highly agreeable in the heat waves of summer. Furniture generally occupies little space in rooms arranged in Japanese style: tables and chairs fold away and can be stored in cupboards out of sight. In contrast, in more modern rooms furniture is permanently left out. However it is becoming increasingly common to find a cupboard standing in a corridor and Western style furniture encroaching on a room covered with Tatami. These are concessions that Japanese taste has been forced to make to modernism. Increasingly the mechanized, utilitarian, sometimes ugly aspects of the modern world intrude upon the warm intimacy and comfort that has always characterized the Japanese house, a haven of peace, safeguarding its inhabitants from the hustle and bustle of life outside.

*Portrait of Sanyutei Encho, by Kaburagi
Kiyokata, 1930. National Museum of
Modern Art, Tokyo.*

The Psychology of the Japanese Today

Japan's image today is of an extraordinarily complex society, in which traditional values co-exist with modern civilization, the two being closely bound up with one another. An extraordinary mirror of the West, Japanese life remains nonetheless strongly hierarchical in all its aspects, whether religious, social or economic. Its hierarchical spirit is a direct inheritance from the feudalism of the Kamakura period in the thirteenth century, which was in no way changed by the Meiji revolution (1868). Underlying the whole of Japanese society, the true core of Japan, incarnated in the spirit of the Samurai, is still unchanged, albeit that the lord of bygone days is now a powerful company director, and his high-ranking henchmen (Juyaku) are the managing directors of modern times. Company executives are, in their turn, the Samurai of today, and employees the ordinary soldiers.

But management in Japan also involves obtaining the co-operation of top or middle-ranking staff. A prodigious hierarchy, yes, but based on the well-known principle of consensus, in other words, assent and analysis of decisions.

One can generally say that Japan as a whole operates on the consensus principle. In practice this explains not only the unswerving loyalty of the employee to his superiors and his total identification with the company, but also the general loyalty to the man who is the embodiment of the very soul of Japan, that is to say the Emperor. To the extent that the Emperor is the direct descendant of the original Shinto gods, Izanagi and Izanami, his person, like the Japanese land itself, is sacred.

It is important to understand the extent to which the sacred nature of Japan determines the country's entire structure, with all its subtleties, not because the Japanese are essentially religious, but simply because the first religion of Japan consists, if one may venture to say so, in being Japanese above all else. In brief, all Japanese belong first and foremost to one entity, that of Japan itself, which remains always the land of the gods, and in a certain sense all Japanese continue to belong to the same family, that of the original couple (Izanagi-Izanami), of whom they are in a manner of speaking distant cousins.

This also explains why, notwithstanding appearances, modern Japan seems to be an impregnable fortress where strangers, whoever they might be, are tolerated, but have virtually no chance of being permanently and properly integrated into the country's life. To be born Japanese is perhaps, as Professor Tsunoda explains, to have a brain whose left and right sections do not function separately, as in all other brains, but together as a single entity. Professor Tadao Umesao, the well-known anthropologist, tells us that if it were possible for a Westerner to read the inside of a Japanese brain, he would be as surprised as if he had suddenly met a Martian. There is indeed a mystery to Japan, in the sense that Westerners neither hold the key to nor have the culture to understand all the complexities of a mind and of a sensibility which is in every respect disconcerting.

One can in effect accumulate the paradoxes of the Japanese mind, present them in one light, or indeed in quite the opposite one. The two analyses will in practice complement each other and show a new reality. The Japanese are at the same time pragmatic and irrational; not mystical, but strongly bound to aspects of religion; pagan and profane, while always preserving their sense of the sacred; efficient, and also tied to ancient superstitions. Their individualism is an emanation of group spirit, their toughness is rivalled only by an almost exacerbated sensitivity and emotivity, like an expression of a double nature, as much feminine as masculine. The solitary spirit of the Samurai is an apt reflection of this. The sense of the fragility of all things, of impermanence and transience, symbolized by the cult of the cherry blossom, is associated to a certain insensitivity, indeed a cruel hardness, when duty and obedience require it.

Another mysterious aspect of the Japanese people concerns the continuity of their culture and behavior throughout the course of history. In 239 Queen Himiko sent a first mission to China. For centuries and centuries Japan was profoundly influenced by Chinese culture. Doubtless this was born of historical necessity, much as in modern times Japan was obliged to open itself to the West, but in neither case, whether towards China or the West, has Japan shown the slightest gratitude. In effect, the Japanese mind has unusually versatile powers of assimilation; it adapts, but it also considerably transforms and recreates from within what it has taken from outside. This is the character of the people's genius, capable from every point of view of research, insatiably curious about the civilizations that surround it. Today this curiosity has applied itself to strategy and through it Japan has kept extraordinarily well abreast of all that goes on in the world, in particular in the fields of advanced technology, science and economy. For its own part, however, Japan remains to a large extent a proud and closed fortress. Which leads Professor Tadao Umesao to say that Japan is like a black hole into which everything goes and nothing comes out. This situation serves, on the other hand, to protect the essentially subtle qualities of the Japanese mind and culture. Based on a sense of harmony and of man's cosmic relation to a Whole of which he is but a living part, Japanese culture conversely introduces the ineffable and inexpressible aspects of this Whole into all aspects of life. One thus finds a highly complementary association between forms of art, architecture, martial arts, gardens and music which, in their different ways, express a constant relationship with this harmony. From it springs an understanding of form, movement and structure, coupled with a particular sense of time and space. All things have a center, which produces a vibration, which creates a link between man and the center, which gives rise to another center, and so on, indefinitely, in the image of the universe. The art that goes into building a little wooden house, a tea room, a shrine, or into shaping a clay vase, is always the expression of a rapid, simple and spontaneous burst of creativity which, in a certain sense, introduces existence itself, and all the harmony that it represents, into the least of its manifestations. Thus time and space are defined in a single word: MA. MA indicates the space or interval between two things. In its applications MA is harmony, certainly, but also a source of efficiency. In the martial arts the space between two adversaries is called Maai. He who has an exact understanding of this space can become an invincible fighter. In similar fashion the Japanese garden is a place whose forms, at the same time free and restrained, spontaneous and controlled, express the subtle and hidden tensions of the soul. All things in effect have their different levels, like the interior of an interior, where the visible and the invisible are closely associated. A perfect example is the famous Ryoan-ji garden which is in a Zen temple in Kyoto. There are fifteen rocks in the garden and from wherever you look at them, one always remains hidden. This is a symbol of the play on reality represented by the concept *Mie-gakure*, which means "seen and hidden."

One might ask oneself if, behind the prodigious Japanese expansion, there is not in existence more than an apparently implacable structure, a dimension that the West has perhaps lost. It is beyond the scope of a few pages, even indeed a book, to give more than a few insights into what one can call invisible Japan. When a businessman leaves his office, he goes home to find himself in a typically Japanese setting. He puts on a *hakama*, a broad and ample garment allowing him freedom of movement. Having served him tea, his wife attends him while he has a hot bath, after which he will converse with her or entertain friends. But once he has crossed his own threshold, it is out of the question to discuss work or office problems. Another life begins, another sensitivity is at play, like a different music. Paradoxically, every morning the Japanese can sing a song to his company, standing at attention, but as soon as he returns home things fall into their natural place. The harmony of existence, which embraces the irrational as much as the rational, is restored. What we call good sense is to the Japanese the "feeling of what is," or "balance," and this balance, that is to say the center of one's sense of being present at everything one does, is to be found as much in the art of preparing tea as in that of inventing and launching a new product. There is no self-mastery unless inner freedom also exists. If the Japanese people did not have a profound feeling for life and nature, which in social and religious life is translated into the innumerable feasts which in their way keep time with the seasons and events of the year, it is certain that efficiency would not exist amidst this kind of constant flowering, where the inner spiritual life, and also the Dionysian sensual life, find free expression.

One cannot then describe Japan without incessantly referring to its cultural aspects. Certainly the modern Japanese towns, hurriedly constructed after the war, seem entirely to contradict the image of an invisible and perhaps ideal Japan. But if it is true that the worst taste is too often associated with the most exquisite, the Japanese are deeply conscious that this loss of equilibrium is but temporary. Tomorrow's Japan is undoubtedly a futuristic vision. And yet, as conceived in the huge project of Tange Kenzo, the most famous of Japanese architects, the town of the future will integrate all traditional concepts. His scheme to build a city of five million inhabitants in the Bay of Tokyo is particularly bold and fantastic. In drawing its inspiration from the development of the human embryo, the town will resemble a cellular unity, its backbone a three-level system of roads and communications, in which one will find in practice the concepts of MA, that is to say Japanese time and space.

146. *BAN-GASA. A special waxed paper umbrella used with kimonos during the rainy season.*

147-148. *AMA. Women diving for pearls, from Honshu. These women are completely clothed, while the Ama from Kyushu dive topless.*

149. *IREZUMI. A tattoo parlor for members of Yakusa or crime gangs. There are several known gangs, but Yamaguchi-Gumi is the largest, with thousands of members.*

150. *A particularly splendid example. They say that when these men die they are skinned and the tattooed skin is preserved by their relatives.*

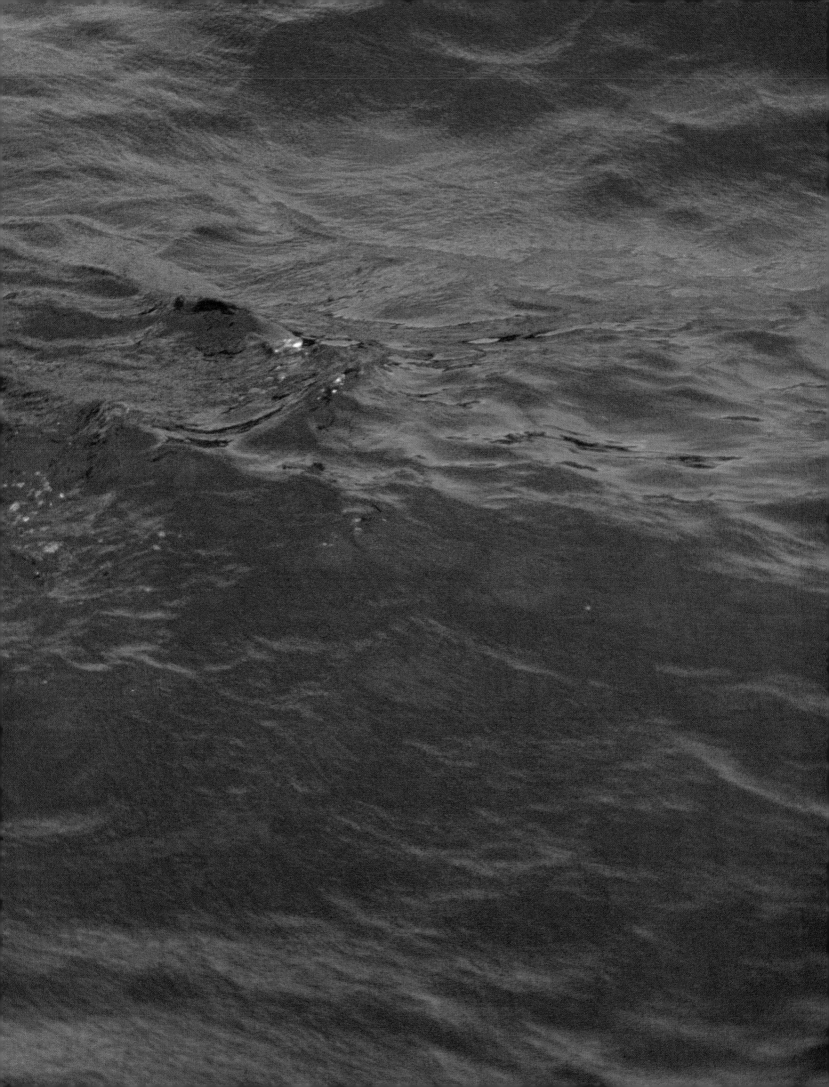

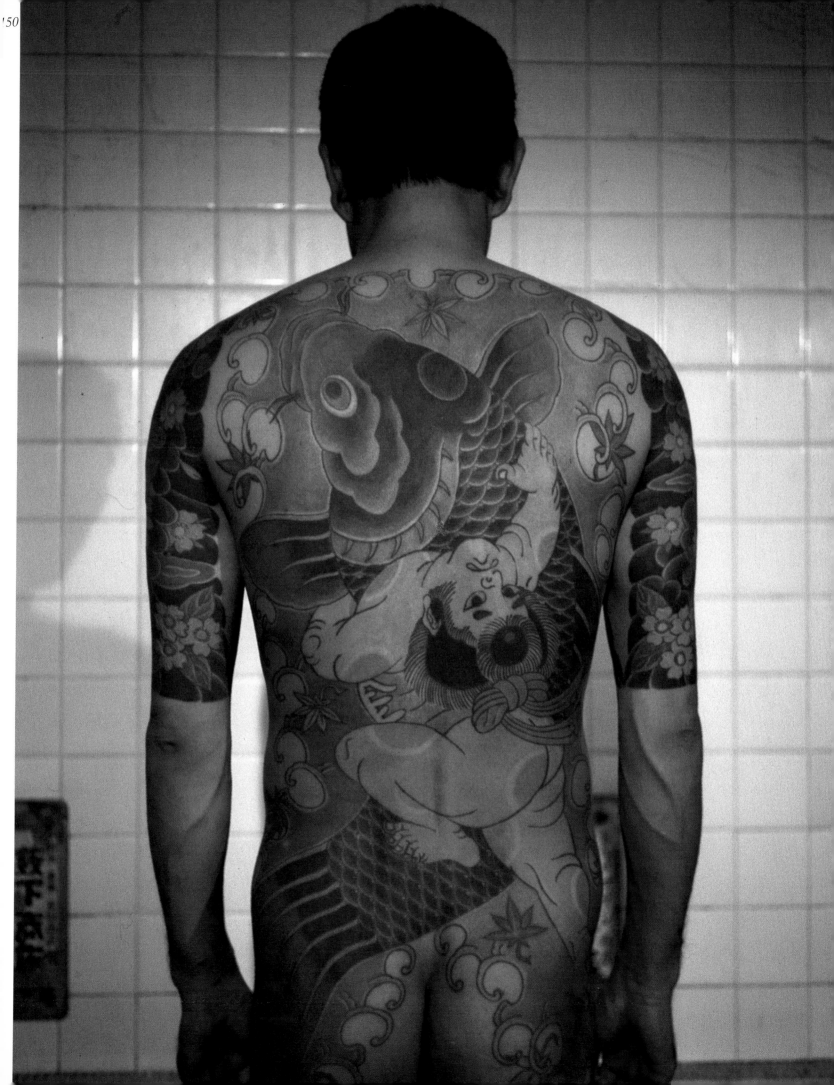

151

151. *HAKA-MAIRI. Prayer for the souls of
the dead in the cemetery.*

152. *Preparing for O-Bon ceremony:
calling the souls of the dead.*

153. *A thousand lanterns in a Kyoto
cemetery.*

154. *IZUMOYA RESTAURANT
(Shijo-Kamogawa, in Kyoto). Menu and
prices vary according to the level of the
building. The lower floors have the
simplest food and the lowest prices. The
style and the costs rise as one goes higher.*

155

156

155-156. Preparing the fire, and sword making or Katana-koji, one of Japan's most ancient and traditional handcrafts. The sword itself was regarded as an almost mystical object in ancient Japan. The rights attached to wearing it, the deeds it performed, the fame and honors bestowed on an expert swordsman, all these contributed to giving the Katana itself a distinction that is hard for us to imagine. Most historians see the year 1596 as a time of fundamental change when the Koto (old sword) gave way to the Shinto (new sword). Throughout Japanese history the restrictions of sword wearing were strictly enforced. Most swordsmen were Samurai, although occasionally outsiders were allowed to wear one, but never two swords. The early Japanese curved sword was worn as the Tachi, slung from the waist with the edge downwards and used from horseback. As early as the twelfth century a curved sword with the edge up was carried by foot soldiers and then adapted for mounted Samurai. The sword

makers who were, and are, expert craftsmen care as much for beauty of texture and temper line as for practical effectiveness.

157. YUZEN NAGASHI. Rinsing dyed cloth in a river.

158. TOSA INU. Fighting dog. This sport originated in Tosa province, Shikoku, early in the century. The dogs are classified by weight and performance and betting is heavy for the best known fighters.

159. TSUNOKIRI. Cutting the horns of a deer.

160

160. *KOKESHI-KUKURI. Making wooden dolls.*

161. *HATAORI. Making cloth.*

162. *CHA-NO-YU (way of tea). Tea ceremony; a full ceremony takes nearly an entire day. The original teahouses were built in gardens in a simple, rustic style incorporating as many natural elements in the building as possible.*

163. *NI-JO Castle garden, in Kyoto.*

164. *Selling Mizubue (water birds) in Hakone.*

163

164

165

165. At the fish market.

166. Preparing tuna for canning in Tokyo.

167. *FURUHON MATSURI. One of Japan's
many book fairs; this one specializes in old
books.*

Cultural Heritage

Japan has a long tradition in all fields of the arts, going back at least as far as the sixth century A.D. The artistic treasures that the country jealously conserves, classified by the government as "national treasures" and "important cultural works," are scattered throughout the provinces, in the safe-keeping of private families, Shinto shrines, Buddhist temples and other institutions. As a result the State museums are relatively poor and often borrow the works they wish to put on public display, varying the theme of their exhibitions each time. This of course excludes large monuments which cannot be moved and must be visited in situ. Nonetheless it is worth pointing out that the oldest museum in the world is in Japan: the Shoso-in, built of wood, has miraculously survived in Nara since the eighth century, housing three thousand objects which date from the time of its foundation. But unfortunately it is open to the public only once a year, at the beginning of October.

Painting

Apart from the paintings adorning the interior of the great mausoleums (Kofun) of the fourth to fifth centuries, the first pictorial works in Japan imitated Chinese models of the Tang period and central Asian art. This is true both of portraits and the more frequently occurring illustrations of Buddhist texts which, having been imported from China or Korea, were from the seventh or eighth century copied in great number by professional artists, generally Buddhist monks, organized by the highly official "office of paintings" (Edokoro) which had its headquartes in the monasteries of the capital, at that time Heijo-kyo (Nara). The paintings were executed on various materials, paper, hemp cloth, wood panels, with China ink and brilliantly colored. Sometimes the colors were touched up with bird feathers or the wing cases of beetles. Fabrics were also painted and dyed using stencils or wax. Painted works remained a rarity, however, reserved for the use of the court.

In the ninth century the founding of a new capital at Heian-kyo (Kyoto) and the emergence of new Buddhist sects originating from China, was to lay the ground for a flowering of the visual arts. Painting at this time was purely religious in subject matter, for the monasteries were in great need of representations of the divinities and of mandalas to decorate the monastery walls, and the art of the fresco had been abandoned, although it had occasionally been practised at an earlier date (in the Kondo of the Horyu-ji, for example). Paintings were done on silk cloth with China ink and highlighted with gold and silver. The Buddhist sutras, brought back in increasingly large number from China by

168. Family portrait at wedding in Shinto shrine.

monks, were systematically copied and illustrated by groups of artists attached to the monasteries and working exclusively for them. Some of the monk-painters began to show a certain originality, notably in their sketches in China ink (sumi-e), breaking away from their Chinese models. The fashion for religious portraits, also imported from China, began to develop, but the Japanese artists had not as yet acquired the skills of their masters and produced flat and lifeless works.

It was only from the tenth and eleventh centuries that painting developed, with the advent of more popular Buddhist sects, such as the Amida, and the establishment of a brilliant court by the Fujiwara regents. Two distinct styles of painting were to emerge from this period, Kara-e, which was influenced by Chinese painting, and Yamato-e, which took its inspiration from Japanese life. The Yamato-e painters decorated the houses of the nobility, palaces, a variety of temples, with innumerable murals, painted doors and screens, and secular representations of the work of the months, the seasons, landscapes, and so forth. The romances of the period began to be illustrated on calligraphed scrolls (e-makimono). Drawing was then free-hand and presented its subject as if viewed from above, the artist's eye beholding the scene from the rooftops. Faces were simplified, stereotyped, and the accent was on the extreme richness of the costumes. Towards the end of the Fujiwara period (twelfth century) illustrated scrolls, secular or religious in subject (temple history, for example) represented series of scenes executed in ink with a flexible brush and depicting episodes of everyday life with great realism and even humor. Some of these paintings were simply uncolored drawings, perhaps intended to feed the first printing presses (carved blocks of wood) which, although wood engraving had been imported from Korea in the eighth century, did not develop until the end of the period. The great novels or romances were then illustrated, most significantly the Genji-monogatari, as well as a variety of stories and tales no longer written to edify but simply to amuse. One of the most celebrated painters of the eleventh century was apparently Kose Hirotaka, whose work is a good example of Yamato-e art. In the genre of caricature, one must mention Toba Sojo, who shows a caustic humor in his caricatures of animals and birds (Choju Giga), which are presented rather like a cartoon strip. The art of calligraphy, regarded as noble and virtuous, was associated to painting and from then on became a part of it. The Chinese-inspired Kara-e school gradually disappeared and Japanese painting became resolutely national.

The rise to power of the warrior classes during the Kamakura period (1192-1333) and the growing prominence of the new Buddhist sects prompted painting to develop through a skillful mingling of Chinese elements and Japanese inspiration. Though temple paintings were made to come alive and continued to be richly colored, the fashion turned to realistic portraiture, sometimes modeled on the Song period in China, and the resulting pictures were lively and dynamic.

E-makimono came very much into vogue and readily depicted scenes of battle and everyday life in the court and monasteries, showing great attention to detail, as much in the attitude of the figures as in the background setting, and often tending to caricature. Religious paintings, in treating of monastic buildings, seized the opportunity to portray landscapes which often became predominant. All techniques were explored: paintings were done in China ink or gouache, on silk or paper, sometimes monochrome or lightly colored, often fully illuminated. Their subject matter was equally wide-ranging: portraits of monks, emperors and warriors, images of the gods, genre painting, illustrations of stories and historical chronicles, faithfully depicting the manners of the age.

The Muromachi period (1333-1582) witnessed a radical change in artistic inspiration with the revival of contacts with China and the growing importance of the Zen sects. The Suiboku style of painting then came very much to the fore, imitating Chinese art, but in a spirit that was determinedly Japanese: the stroke of the paintbrush became all important, striving to express the essential nature of things, to suggest rather than realistically depict them. Painters began to specialize (bamboos, travel-scapes, portraits, poems) and Chinese Suiboku was Japanized, successfully adopting the technique of Haboku, or retouched wash drawings. The painter Sesshu (1420-1506) and the Soga school continued to develop the style of the "three friends" (No-ami, Gei-ami and So-ami) and of Shubun (fourteenth-fifteenth century). Yamato-e art was not in the meantime neglected and painters of this school continued to work on religious subjects: their various styles were drawn together in the work of Tosa Mitsunobu (1434-1525), who was one of the last of his school. At the end of the fifteenth century a new style emerged, inspired both by Zen and Yamato-e painting. Its first practitioner was Kano Mitsunobu (1434-1530) who used the Suiboku technique to treat subjects of Chinese or Buddhist inspiration in a typically Japanese style. He was imitated by his son Kano Motonobu (1476-1559) who put color into wash drawings. Calligraphy continued to be an integral part of painting, but broke little new ground, content to copy Song and Yuan models.

The following period, the Momoyama (1582-1603), was to witness the disappearance of monastic schools of painting, the monasteries having been destroyed by Nobunaga and Hideyoshi. This was the period of the great castles. Instead of edifying or descriptive paintings, the Daimyo wanted works which would decorate their palaces and the screens that furnished them. Kano Eitoku (1543-1590) and the painters of his school developed Sumi-e painting on gold and silver backgrounds, combining purely decorative art (*Shoheki-ga*) with the principles of Yamato-e. The other painters of the Kano family, Takanobu, Hidenobu, Naganobu, Sanraku and Yoshinobu, among others, working for the powerful of the time, carried out innumerable decorations of screens and fans and illustrated historical scrolls and hanging pictures (*Kakemono*) with felicitous results, handling a wide range of subjects in a manner both sober and decorative. Other painters continued to work in the Suiboku style of the Muromachi period, particularly that of Sesshu, deriving their technique from that of the Chinese painters. Meanwhile a number of them, such as Tawaraya Sotatsu (early seventeenth century), broke away from the old-style Yamato-e by illustrating literary works in a highly decorative manner, while in Osaka and Sakai another group of artists carried on traditional Yamato-e painting. Towards the end of the period other artists, working primarily for rich traders, painted secular works (flowers, animals, landscapes, genre scenes) specifically to appeal to popular taste.

With the arrival of foreigners in Japan in the middle of the fifteenth century, Western art (Yoga) came to influence a few Japanese artists (perhaps converts to Christianity), leading them to reproduce examples of Portuguese or Dutch art, which they handled in a wholly original manner. The majority of their work consisted of screens (Nanban

Byobu) decorated with scenes portraying foreigners, missionaries, boats, Jesuits. Their paintings were never signed.

The Tokugawa Shoguns of the Edo period (1603-1868) were to favor the traditional schools of painting (Kano, Tosa and others), while the nouveaux riches, traders and bourgeoise preferred more decorative and popular works. The Kano divided into two branches, one based in Kyoto, the other in Edo, the new Shogunal capital. However, the painters of this school, lacking in originality, merely imitated their predecessors and the Chinese. In Kyoto the aristocracy patronized the artists of the Tosa family, who continued to work in Chinese style (Kanga). Some of them made a move to reintroduce the Yamato-e style, but only met with a short-lived success. In Edo, on the other hand, the emulators of Sotatsu developed a very decorative, highly colored style, choosing nature as their principal subject. The great screen paintings of Ogata Korin (1658-1716), his brother Kenzan (1663-1743) and their disciples, such as Sakai Hoitsu (1761-1828), display an extremely modern realism in their decorative approach. Maruyama Okyo (1733-1795), influenced by European painting, produced realistic works and gathered round him in Kyoto a great many painters of varying inspirations, while artists of another group were inspired by the paintings of the Hoku-ga school (in the north) and the Nan-ga school (in the south) of China. These well-lettered painters, who dedicatedly studied the Chinese classics, won themselves a considerable reputation, although they were in many cases amateurs. Yosa Buson (1716-1783), Ike-no-Taiga (1723-1776) in Kyoto, Aoki Mokubei (1767-1833) and Gyokudo (1745-1820) in Osaka, Tani Buncho (1723-1840) in Edo, became famous in this genre, which they revived while giving free reign to their own inspiration.

But painting was hard work and the Chonin (townsmen), who aspired to an artistic life, turned their attentions to a genre up to now regarded as minor: wood-engraving. At first its subject matter was limited: figures of Kabuki actors and courtesans (*Bijin*, or pretty women, the equivalent of pin-ups in our time). These pictures, considered to be reflections of an ephemeral period, were called Ukiyo-e (images of a floating world). Initially these naive works showed little artistic quality and it was only from the end of the eighteenth century that distinct individual styles began to be seen, in the engravings of Suzuki Harunobu (1725-1770), which were multi-colored (Nishiki-e). The portraits of actors, particularly those by Shuncho, Buncho and Sharaku, the engravings of pretty women by Tori Kiyonaga (1752-1815) and Kitagawa Utamaro (1753-1806) began truly to be works of art. Hokusai (1760-1849) and Ando Hiroshige (1797-1858) carried the art of Ukiyo-e to its zenith, the former in his admirable popular drawings (*manga*), the latter in his totally original landscapes. One must also mention the series of scenes and landscapes by Utagawa Kuniyoshi (1797-1858), which are true engravings, in the purest Japanese style.

At the beginning of the Meiji period (1868-1912), the trends of the Edo period continued and, in parallel with Ukiyo-e, now carried out for enthusiasts in the Western world, Japanese painters began to take an interest in European art, notably under the direction of Italian artists. There was also a move in Japan to revive former styles, adapting them to the techniques of oil painting. Every style was tested in the new medium, resulting in a good number of schools: Yokoyama Taikan (1868-1958), Kano Hogai (1828-1888), Okakura Tenshin (1862-1913), Maeda Seison (1885-1977), Tomioka Tessai (1836-1924) are among the

Bugaku dancers, by Tawaraya Sotatsu.
From the Edo period (seventeenth
century). Sanbo-in, Kyoto.

most highly thought of. Their countless disciples ventured into every genre and covered all subjects, some frankly Westernized, others seeking to rediscover a style that was truly Japanese. The majority continued to paint in this way, remarkable for its extreme diversity, throughout the following period, that of Taisho (1912-1926), and even during the Showa period (starting in 1926), until after the war. Since 1950 Japanese artists have traveled, studied in Paris and New York, and integrated into Western schools following modern artistic trends.

Sculpture

Apart from preistoric statuettes and the Haniwa of baked clay which decorate the great burial places of the Kofun period, both isolated artistic developments, Japanese sculpture developed at the same time as painting, under the auspices of Buddhism imported from Korea during the course of the sixth century. This sculpture, which was Buddhist and often monumental, closely followed Korean canons, themselves inspired by the Chinese styles of the Wei or Sui period. Throughout the Asuka (645-710) and the following Nara periods (710-794), bronze was predominant, though quality woods (sandal, camphor) were also much favored. Sculpture reached its peak in the works of Tori, who at the beginning of the seventh century produced admirable temple statuary. Other sculptors drew their inspiration directly from Korea and their representations of the deities, made from wood and covered with gold leaf, were endowed with "archaic" smiles and garments executed in flowing lines. The majority of sculptures of the Asuka period show a strict frontality and are of triangular frame. The figures are elongated, graceful, infused with gentleness. In the Nara period sculptors were more influenced by Tang art. However, they sought to produce works that were original, albeit of Tang inspiration. Bronze statues were cast by the lost wax method. In the case of large works a special technique was employed, the bronze being cast in successive horizontal layers. After the casting of the immense statue of the Buddha Vairocana in the Todai-ji (unveiled in 752), bronze became scarce and artists seemed from then on to prefer clay, wood and lacquer. Volcanic rock was rarely used, proving difficult to chisel. The faces of the sculptures became more realistic, their bodies were stiff and often massive, conferring an immense dignity on the deities they represented. They were also embellished with numerous details. The new techniques imported from China, such as the use of dry lacquer on a base of clay or wood which allowed very free modeling, won favor with sculptors, who, like painters, were generally Buddhist monks, often come from China. Wood statues imitated those in bronze, being lacquered or gilded, and showed a tendency to realism that became increasingly marked, reaching its culmination in the Kamakura period. The sculpture of the Heian period was almost entirely in wood, since the dry lacquer technique was progressively abandoned. But while sculptors had previously worked on single blocks of wood, they now worked on several parts which were afterwards fitted together. This allowed them to carve details. The sculpture of this period tended to Japanize Chinese models, although respecting traditional Buddhist canons in its style. One of the major works of the period was the Amida Buddha in the Byodo-in at Uji, by Jocho and dating from 1050. In Kyoto workshops were set up, in which sculptors worked primarily for the monasteries. Towards the end of the period statues were completely painted, no longer simply gilded.

Statue of Muchaku (Asanga) by Unkei,
from the Kamakura period (1208).
Kofuku-ji Temple, Nara.

It was in the Kamakura period that sculpture reached its culminating point in Japan. Inspired by the warlike spirit at large in the country, sculptors produced works that were powerful, dynamic and often of a gripping realism. To make their figures more lifelike they gave them glass eyes and painted them in natural colors. Wood was used almost always, and the art of portraiture reached one of its high points. Bronze was used only for Buddhist statues which were executed in the Chinese Tang style: the great Buddha of Kamakura (1252) is one of the best known examples. Among the best sculptors of this period one must cite Unkei, his son Tankei, Kankei and their descendants. At the end of the period and when this great line of sculptors had died out, the art declined sharply in Japan. In the Muromachi period it was scarcely represented, except in the form of Noh masks. So sculpture fell into disfavor and the few works still produced were but pale reflections of those of bygone days. During the Edo period sculptors were totally lacking in imagination. Their works were mere copies of the past, overladen with ornamentation and paint, imitating Chinese sculptures of the Ming dynasty. Only the names of isolated artists are worthy of note, for example the monk Enku (died in (1696) who carved his statues out of pinewood with an axe, or Tankai (1629-1717). Sculptors preferred to turn their skills to making dolls or Netsuke, little objects which at times displayed a real talent on the part of their makers. At first purely utilitarian (they were used for keeping little articles in one's belt), Netsuke were rediscovered at the end of the nineteenth century by collectors in the West.

Literature

Literature started in Japan with official historical compilations, the *Kojiki* and the *Nihon Shoki*, whose purpose was to establish the legitimacy of the emperors, at the beginning of the eighth century. Beforehand there had only existed invocations to the Kami (divinities) of the soil, and *Norito*, handed down to us in anthologies, such as that of *Manyoshu*, compiled around 760, which preserves all the Japanese poetry, religious, peasant and courtly, of the fifth to eighth centuries. Further anthologies were then put together, in both the Japanese and Chinese tongues (*Kaifuso* of 751), as well as collections of stories showing a clear Buddhist influence (*Nihon Ryoi-ki*, early ninth century). During the Heian period other poetry anthologies followed, such as the *Kokin-shu*, composed of *Waka*, traditional poems. Then in the tenth century the first proper stories appeared, such as "The Tale of the Bamboo Cutter" (*Taketori-monogatari*), and accounts of travels (*Nikki*). Among the forerunners of the true novel one must mention, from the same century, "The Tale of the Hollow Tree" (*Utsubo-monogatari*), "The Tale of the Cave" (*Ochikubo-monogatari*) and a few *Nikki*. The first great Japanese novel was undoubtedly the *Genji-monogatari*, written around the year 1000 by a court lady, Murasaki Shikibu. It was the very long and very complicated story of prince Genji and his son Kaoru. The style, which is extremely flowing, evokes the sentiments of the period in Kyoto court circles and minutely describes the goings on, costumes and customs. Sei Shonagon, another court lady, in her *Makura-no Soshi* (Pillow Book), gives us a series of personal impressions, randomly inspired, often malicious, always apposite. The *Nikki* were not abandoned as a literary form and in them a number of ladies gave expression to their emotions, their joy, their suffering in their travels: examples are the intimate journals of Murasaki Shikibu, of Izumi

Shikibu, of the author of *Sarashina-nikki*, all noble ladies of the eleventh century. The vogue for *monogatari* became widespread and a good many authors ventured into this genre, more or less imitating the *Genji-monogatari*. At the same period edifying stories made an appearance, influenced by Buddhism, for example *Konjaku-monogatari*, consisting of innumerable anecdotes "of bygone days," and collections of stories, such as *Uji-Shui-monogatari*. With the advent of warriors in the Kamakura period epic romances developed, recounting the noble deeds of warriors in both old and recent times: the *Eiga-monogatari*, the *O-Kagami* (Great Mirror), the *Azuma-Kagami* (Mirror of the East) are characteristic examples. Next came veritable historic chronicles, generally devoted to the period of the establishment of the Shogunate, such as the *Hogen-monogatari*, the *Heike-monogatari*, then the *Taiheiki* (fourteenth century), in which fiction is often mingled with reality. Poetry did not lose ground in the meantime and further anthologies saw the light of day, compiled by authors such as Fujiwara no Teika (1162-1241) or Minamoto no Sanetomo. The tradition of travel journals (*Nikki*) was maintained in the *Izayoi-nikki* of Lady Abutsu-ni, as also that of "notes as the pen flows," the best known examples being the *Hojo-ki* by Kamo no Chomei (1153-1216) and the *Tsurezure-gusa* (In the Course of Boredom) by Kenko Hoshi (1283-1350), to some extent imitating the *Makura no Soshi*. The fourteenth century also saw the birth of Noh theater, which developed from a combination of peasant dances and Buddhist philosophies. Its texts, the majority of which were by Kan'ami and his son Ze'ami (1363-1443), brought about a revival of the poetic genre. These *Yokyoku* are long rhyming poems interspersed with dialogue, working more to evoke an aesthetic feeling than to tell a story. In the intervals of the Noh plays, farces called *Kyogen* were inserted, short verse tales closely resembling the fabliaux of medieval France. The Edo period brought the rise of a more popular form of literature, the *Soshi*, recounting stories of love and of miracles, heroic legends, animal tales, and so on. These stories were sometimes written in the *Kana* syllabary so that the people could understand them (hence their name, *Kana-soshi*). In the mid sixteenth century *Joruri*, the book of puppet plays, came increasingly into vogue and from it, under the impetus of Chikamatsu Monzemon and Gidayu, developed Kabuki theater. Chikamatsu's output was vast and ranged from historical drama to the simple telling of an item of news. This Japanese Shakespeare tackled every genre and was imitated by all his successors. At the same time a "scientific" literature developed, undertaking the study of Japanese and Chinese letters in a predominantly moralistic spirit, as seen in the work of Hayashi Doshun (1585-1657) and Kaibara Ekiken (1630-1714) or the historian Arai Hakuseki (1657-1725).

A new genre came to enrich Japanese poetry, namely the *Haiku*, which reached its fullest expression in the work of Basho around 1660. In three short lines it managed to recreate a world, evoking sounds, sensations, fleeting impressions: the Haiku is a kind of photograph of a privileged moment. This poetic genre came so much into vogue that to this very day there are few Japanese who have not tried it. With the return to "national" studies, principally brought about by the work of Motoori Norinaga (1730-1801) and Ueda Akinari (1734-1809), the Edo period witnessed the growing success of romantic and fantastical literature, evidenced by the *Yomihon* (books to read) which were both cheap and aimed at a popular readership. Ueda Akinari, Santo Kyoden (1761-1816), Takarai Bakin (1767-1848) rendered the genre illustrious, dealing above all with noble subjects. These works, which had literary pretentions, were quickly followed by a series of other cheap novels (the *Kusa-soshi*, the *Share-bon*) which, while better adapted to the townsmen's tastes, were at times openly vulgar. Next to this enormous production, the *Kokkei-bon*, or comic novels, stand out. After 1868 young writers turned to the study of the West, published political and technical works and discovered European literature. Some sought to imitate (or were influenced by) French, English and German authors, others tried to bring their national literature to the fore. Fukuzawa Yukichi (1835-1901) was one of the pioneers of the study of European civilizations, while others, such as Kanagaki Robun (1829-1894) devoted themselves to a more "committed" literature, intended to uphold the Meiji government. Yet others tackled the political novel, for example Yano Fumio (1850-1931), whose *Keikoku-bidan* recounts the struggles of the Thebans against Sparta. However, the young writers of the early twentieth century preferred a literature free from the constraints of social and political issues. One of their number was Tsubouchi Shoyo (1859-1935) who advocated a more psychological and more scientifically constructed form of novel. Fatabatei Shimei (1861-1909), Ozaki Koyo (1867-1903), Koda Rohan (1867-1947) were the first representatives of this new movement. They were soon followed by writers from literary circles, such as Kitamura Tokoku (1868-1894), Shimazaki Toson (1872-1943), Tokutomi Roka (1868-1927) who belonged to the Romantic movement. Nagai Kafu (1879-1959), for his part, took his inspiration from Zola. The above were soon opposed by writers of a new Naturalist school, for example Kunikida Doppo (1871-1908), Tayama Katai (1872-1930) and above all Iwano Homei (1873-1920). Meanwhile, aside from the Romantic, Realist and Naturalist movements, two major writers prefigured modern literature: Mori Ogai (1862-1922) and Natsume Soseki (1867-1916) whose works sought to stir readers to think about the psychological or other problems that concerned them. Literary reviews helped launch new literary movements and ideas, enthusiastically followed by an entire generation of new writers, such as Mushakoji Saneatsu, Shiga Naoya, Arishima Takeo, all born at the end of the nineteenth century. In parallel, a "proletarian" literature developed, represented by Kobayashi Takiji (1903-1933). Akutagawa Ryunosuke (1892-1982) was a follower of Soseki's literary school, while other authors, such as Tanizaki Junichiro (1896-1965) remained resolutely loyal to the Japanese spirit in what it still retained of its most traditional elements. In place of the "diabolism" of his early manner, Tanizaki then adopted a pessimistic tone, responding to the progressive disappearance of all that had been "his" Japan. Other writers such as Shimazaki Toson wrote long novels of historical and social content.

After the Second World War, a new generation of writers made their name testifying to their experiences (Noma Hiroshi, Shiina Rinzo, Ooka Shohei, etc.), while Dazai Osamu, writing in isolation, displayed a desperate pessimism: he committed suicide in 1948. Kawabata Yasunari then took up the torch of "Japanese" writing, adopting a style of extreme elegance, heavy with symbolism. Mishima Yukio (1925-1970) is revealed in his writings, which are very Westernized, and owes a good measure of his fame to his spectacular suicide. But other writers, more authentically Japanese, came gradually to the fore, such as Oe Kenzaburo, Ishihara Shintaro or, more recently, Inoue Yasushi, Abe Kobo or Takami Jun, to name but a few of them.